Self-catering Italy

HELENA RAMSAY

Illustrated by Penny Quested

HarperCollins*Publishers*

New York
London and Glasgow

The Author
Helena Ramsay has lived in Italy on and off for the past twelve years,
and is now a frequent visitor with her young family. Her previous
publications include *Italian Gardens: A Visitors Guide* (written
with her husband), *The Girl in the Apple: A Tuscan Fairytale*
and *Advice at Cost Price* (for the National Association of
Citizens Advice Bureaux).

Edited and designed by the Book Creation Company Limited,
1 Newburgh Street, London W1V 1LH

Series concept: Jackie Jones
Editors: Eileen Cadman, Sydney Francis
Design: Christine Wood
Index: Hilary Bird
Research: Emma Hurd, David Johnston
Typesetting: Columns, Reading
Printed in Hong Kong

Published by HarperCollins*Publishers*

The Book Creation Company wishes to thank the following
for their invaluable help: Sulie Bruzzo, Annibale Osti, Valeria Grilli,
Jennie Condie, Helen Sutton, Gianfranca Shepheard,
First Edition Limited.

© Book Creation Company and Jackie Jones 1991
All rights reserved
No part of this work may be reproduced or utilized in any form
by any means, electronic or mechanical, including photocopying,
recording or by any information storage and retrieval system,
without the prior written permission of the publisher.

British Library Cataloguing in Publication Data
Ramsay, Helena
Italy. – (Collins self-catering)
1.Italy. Visitors' guides
I. Title
914.504929

ISBN 0-00-436105-9

While every care has been taken in the preparation of this book,
neither the author nor publishers can accept any liability
for any consequence arising from the use of information
contained herein.

CONTENTS

CHAPTER ONE

INTRODUCTION

It's hard to beat Italy for a truly memorable holiday. The climate, the food and the people are all wonderful. Whether you go as a family or with friends, you're bound to return to Britain wanting to go again.

Italy has been unified as a nation for just over 130 years, and it is still notable for its regional variations – in food, climate and language. Some say that the North and the South are still two different countries. As a tourist, you can take advantage of these differences and see whichever side of Italy suits your taste. The northern regions offer a slightly cooler climate in the summer (although still hot!) while the southern regions are uncompromisingly scorching in midsummer. The North is fairly industrialized in places, although still with history and culture to satisfy the most determined culture-vulture, while the South is still quite traditional and generally poorer – which may appeal more to those who want a rest from modern city life. The islands of the South – Sicily and Sardinia in particular – have a breathtaking beauty and fascination all their own.

Eating different food and eating well is part of the fun of going abroad for a holiday. In Italy, this is easy to do whether you eat at home or eat out – the ingredients and the way they're prepared are usually extremely simple, giving Italian food a classic quality which will probably influence your own cooking ever after.

HOW TO USE THIS BOOK

You'll find that *Self-catering in Italy* is useful at all stages of thinking about your holiday: making plans and organizing; travelling; and once you get there.

The first few chapters will help you during the preparatory stages. Chapter 2 describes self-catering in Italy in a general way. A brief guide to the different regions is followed by a description of the types of self-catering accommodation available, how much they're likely to cost, and what facilities are likely to be (or not be) provided. There's also a special section for those with children. Chapter 3 (MAKING PLANS) covers the various ways of finding a suitable self-catering property, and includes an extensive (but not exhaustive) list of companies that offer self-catering holidays in Italy. The pros and cons of the various travel options are also discussed. Chapter 4 (GETTING READY) lists everything you need to think about when preparing to travel abroad – passports, insurance, currency, health – with useful checklists of items that it's easy to forget.

The book then moves on to what you can expect when you arrive (WELCOME TO ITALY, Chapter 5). It describes what happens when you take possession of a self-catering property, and includes useful phrases and vocabulary.

Chapter 6 (EATING AND DRINKING) approaches the heart of the self-catering holiday with a description of Italian habits and customs concerning food and drink. The range of beverages (both alcoholic and non-alcoholic) is described, followed by a trip through the various types of Italian eatery and what they serve – for the times when you'd rather eat out.

Chapter 7 (SHOPPING FOR FOOD) will give you an excellent start to the adventure of shopping (take this book with you when you go). It provides a detailed description of the shops and markets, and the type of food you'll find in them. The whole range of food is discussed – dairy products, vegetables, meat, fish, groceries, and so on – with tips on how the Italians cook some of them. Chapter 8 is the core of the book for self-caterers. A wide range of simple menus is suggested (with the shopping list in Italian alongside), including meals which need almost no preparation and only require a visit to the local shop. Eating like the locals doesn't mean spending hours and hours in the kitchen.

A big worry for some people can be taking children: Will they eat the food? How do restaurants react to them? Can you get nappies? Chapter 9 will reassure you on these points, and provides other practical information about taking children.

The following chapters – with sections on housekeeping, survival shopping, local services and health – are packed with advice and information on how to keep problems to a minimum, and what to do when things *do* go wrong. Since most self-caterers are likely to have a car, the section on driving gives basic information about the Italian rules of the road, and what to do if your car breaks down.

Although you're going on holiday to get away from it all, it may be necessary for you to keep in touch with friends or relatives at home. There's a section on how to make sure that you can be contacted, and how you can contact them if necessary.

While this book strives to be optimistic, it's as well to be prepared in case of emergencies, and Chapter 12 provides brief but necessary practical information about how to cope if one arises. On a happier note, you'll probably want to bring back something to remind you of your trip, and Chapter 13 gives a general description of the enormous variety of things you can buy.

SPEAKING ITALIAN

Some people, when planning a trip abroad, rush out and buy the language book and tapes, religiously practise the first three lessons, then put them away and never refer to them again. It's not necessary to do a crash-course in Italian unless you want to. Even on a self-catering holiday, you can get by with the basics. This book includes easy, useful phrases to give you confidence in a variety of situations but apart from these, if you don't have time or energy to do more, all you need to do is learn the courtesies (please, thank-you) and the numbers – it's much more soporific than counting sheep at night. With these committed to memory, you'll be able to understand and make yourself understood (more or less) when shopping – prices, amounts, measurements – and in other practical situations which require knowledge of telephone numbers, or times of planes and trains.

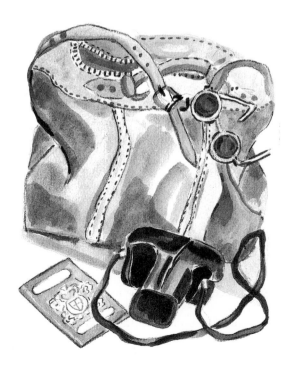

CHAPTER TWO

THINKING OF GOING

Italy has been a popular holiday retreat for the British for a very long time. The Italian Riviera, Tuscany, with its beautiful landscape, and Rome, Italy's capital city with its wealth of historical and artistic treasures, are familiar British stamping grounds. However, Italy also has other attractions that will repay inspection.

If you want a lazy holiday flopping on the beach, the endless Italian coastline provides plenty of self-catering opportunities. If you like to sample the rich and varied cuisine and delectable wines, then the countryside in one of the northern regions will probably be your choice. The South has often been ignored as a holiday region, but tourists are beginning to discover that it has its own wild beauty.

Self-catering is a way of discovering the country at first hand. You come into contact on a day-to-day basis with ordinary people, which is the best way of finding out what Italy is really like. It used to be the case that, when the British went to Italy, they'd take a mountain of things with them to protect them from the dangers of things foreign – self-catering was a more laborious affair in those days! The modern traveller is much more inclined to experience life as the Italians themselves live it, and this can provide one of the main pleasures of the holiday.

If you're prepared to abandon your inhibitions about trying to communicate in another language, shopping can be part of the adventure. Even a little Italian goes a long way, and you get a tremendous sense of achievement when someone understands what you say! However, self-catering also means that you have your own front door and complete privacy, and it's an economical way of being abroad with children. You can live as you normally would without wondering whether you're bothering other people.

REGION-BY-REGION GUIDE

The Val d'Aosta (Aosta Valley) shares borders with both France and Switzerland. In some areas the people speak French which is recognized as an official second language throughout the region. The mountains are some of the highest in Europe and there are a number of popular ski resorts that generate a good proportion of the region's annual income. Like so many mountainous areas, the Val d'Aosta is very popular with walkers during the summer. When you look at the chalets and the beautiful Alpine landscape it can be difficult to believe that you're in Italy.

Piedmont, literally 'the foot of the mountains', encompasses the foothills of the Alps in the extreme north-west of the country. It shares borders with France and Switzerland and the Piedmontese dialect is drawn from both French and Italian. Some of Italy's best red wines come from here and so do most of the country's white truffles. Piedmontese winters are snowy but it's hot in summer. If you can go to Piedmont in autumn you'll be able to feast off every conceivable variety of wild mushroom.

The Italian Riviera (Liguria) used to draw the rich and famous from all over Europe. Its exceptionally mild winters made it particularly popular with northern Europeans. Those glorious days have passed but Liguria can still offer its visitors a ravishing coastline, a fascinating history and a delicious local cuisine.

To the east, Lombardy occupies the vast, flat agricultural valley of the Po. The landscape is punctuated by rows of poplars and the bright sheen of paddy fields. Much of Italy's silk is produced in the area around Brianza, where the wheat fields are divided by rows of mulberry bushes. The beautiful lakes to the north of Milan are the main tourist attraction of the region. The landscape, with its mountainous backdrop, is reminiscent of Switzerland. The winters are cold and often foggy, but you should expect real heat in the summer.

The snow-capped peaks of the Dolomites provide a dramatic backdrop in the region of Trentino-Alto Adige. Until 1918 The Alto Adige was Austrian, and it still has a distinctly Germanic feel to it – in the province of Bolzano German continues to be the common language. Tourism is very important to the regional economy. Throughout the winter the well organized ski resorts are buzzing with life. In the summer the skiers are replaced by walkers.

The Veneto is the area surrounding Venice – one of the greatest tourist attractions in the world. It's a varied region, combining mountain landscapes with rolling hills, plains, beautiful lakes and valleys. Much of the area is little known to tourists and a holiday here can be characterized by a real sense of discovery. Autumn in the Veneto is particularly beautiful, the early mornings are misty but during the day the countryside is bathed in a rich, golden light.

Friuli-Venezia Giulia is the easternmost region of Italy, and shares a border with both Austria and Yugoslavia. In the areas closest to the border Slovenian or German are the common languages and Trieste, the largest of the Adriatic sea ports, handles more Yugoslavian and Austrian trade than Italian. Food in this region is a fascinating reflection of the multicultural background. Exotic spices are used with an abandon rooted in the area's eastern heritage, while the glorious cakes and pastries are reminiscent of nothing so much as a Viennese coffee shop. Like all of northern Italy, the winters are cold here and the summers hot.

Emilia Romagna, to the south of Lombardy, is one of the most prosperous regions in Italy. Much of the countryside is flat and intensively cultivated, but the region's capital city of Bologna is famous for its ancient university and its culinary delights – and Parma, the Renaissance city of Ferrara, and Ravenna with its famous mosaics, also attract visitors from all over the world. Parmesan cheese, Parma ham, Mortadella sausage, Bolognese sauce and many, many other world famous Italian specialities all come from this area. The summers are hot here and the winters cool and damp.

Further south, Tuscany's beautiful rolling hills and glorious medieval cities represent the essence of Italy to most foreign visitors. Here you'll be able to see some of the greatest Renaissance paintings, drink some of the best wine in the world and walk in landscapes that seem hardly to have changed since the 15th century. Spring and autumn can be very wet but the summer is hot and dry.

To the east of Tuscany, mountains effectively divide the fascinating area of Le Marche in half and isolate it from the rest of Italy. There is no motorway to Le Marche, although one is now slowly being built. Perhaps this is why time seems to have stood still among the rolling hills and medieval cities. It's only on the narrow coastal plain that the modern world has really got a grip. Here industry and tourism thrive side by side – Ancona has become one of the most important Adriatic ports. Naturally, the more mountainous areas experience cold and often snowy winters but the whole region is bathed in summer heat each year.

Umbria, in the centre of Italy, is the only completely landlocked region south of Lombardy. Its peaceful landscape is characterized by gently rolling hills. White wine, olive oil and tourism are some of the most important sources of income in the region. Perugia and St Francis's city of Assisi are the principal tourist centres. Avoid Umbria in winter when it tends to be foggy and wet. In spring the hills are carpeted in wild flowers and in summer you can expect day after day of unbroken heat.

Further south, Abruzzi attracts tourists throughout the year as it has the only ski resorts in the South. L'Aquila – a fascinating mountain settlement – is the provincial city. The climate here is relatively cool, which is particularly enjoyable in summer. Pescara is a modern city on the coast, where the extensive beaches are very popular with tourists.

Rome, or more specifically, the Vatican, has drawn foreign visitors to Latium (Lazio) for centuries. Today the capital city continues to attract hordes of tourists. However, anyone prepared to venture outside the city will find that the lovely, sandy coastline, the volcanic hills, lakes and bare sun-scorched mountains combine to create a fascinating and varied landscape. Summer brings a real, southern heat and the winters are short and mild.

Molise is sandwiched between Abruzzi and Puglia. Agriculture is the chief source of income – although the poor, stony soil dictates that it should provide only the poorest of livings. The landscape is mountainous and the winters are very harsh – the snow has been known to last well into the spring. This is a place to visit in midsummer.

Campania on the west coast is in the heart of the Mezzogiorno (roughly translated as 'the land of the midday sun'). The spectacularly beautiful Amalfi coast to the south of Naples is the main tourist area in this region. Precipitous slopes covered in orange and lemon trees, olives, almonds and vines give way to crystal clear seas. Inland the mountainous countryside offers scope for some real adventures. Seafood is the speciality and the best local wines come from grapes grown on the foothills of Vesuvius. Naples itself is a fascinating city.

To the east once more lies Puglia, probably the most affluent region in the Mezzogiorno. Its largely flat and enormous areas are laid down to olive groves. Olive oil, almonds and wine are the principal products. The beautiful and dramatic coastline of the Gargano is gradually being developed as a tourist centre, but inland you'll find that the modern world has had very little impact. Winter is short in Puglia and the summer is long and blisteringly hot.

Basilicata (Lucania), a somewhat desolate region, is the sun-scorched heart of the Mezzogiorno. Much of the countryside is deserted – generations of poverty have resulted in the mass emigration of its inhabitants. The most fertile area is to the north where the foothills of Mount Vulture – an extinct volcano – are clothed in vineyards and olive groves. Matera, one of the oldest cities in the world, is perhaps the only real tourist attraction in the region.

At the southernmost tip of Italy, at the toe of the boot, lies Calabria. It has a beautiful rugged coastline, reminiscent of Greece. Much of the region is covered by wild mountains, scorched by the powerful Mediterranean heat. Tourism is restricted to the coast where the beautiful landscape is marred only by numerous unfinished modern buildings. Many of these belong to local people forced to emigrate in search of work. Building proceeds at a snail's pace – it's only when the distant owners have a bit of cash to spare that a staircase or even another floor can be added to the home of their dreams.

The island of Sicily lies only 2 miles off the mainland and yet it is in a world of its own. Successive foreign invaders have left traces of their own civilizations over the centuries and these have combined to create the slightly exotic flavour that is now the essence of Sicily. The mountainous landscape is clothed in vineyards, lemon and olive groves. The coastline is rocky and spectacular. The summer heat is powerful and the winters are short.

Sardinia, Sicily's nearest neighbour, is completely different. The population is traditionally considered to be quieter and more reserved. The beautiful landscape is mountainous – beware of the prickly brushwood that makes for such hard going off the beaten track. Spring is the ideal time for a holiday in Sardinia – the hills, mountains and even some of the beaches are clothed in wild flowers. During summer the island is scorched by intense heat.

TYPES OF SELF-CATERING ACCOMMODATION

The type of holiday accommodation that you'll find in Italy will depend largely on the area that you visit. Naturally, seaside apartments and mountain chalets have little in common, so generalizations cannot be made. What follows is a broad outline of the different types of accommodation available in Italy. For details about how to find out more and how to book, see Chapter 3, MAKING PLANS.

PURPOSE-BUILT PROPERTIES

Well established seaside resorts and some of the popular inland areas often have purpose-built self-catering accom-modation for summer letting. This usually takes the form of apartments or little chalets which are sometimes grouped together into a 'village'. The facilities are often good in these places. There may well be a private pool and, if they are by the sea, a stretch of beach may be reserved specially for residents. Many tourist villages have their own shop, bar and restaurant, and some run a regular bus service to the nearest town. You may even find that there is a babysitting service or at least a daytime crèche. If this is important to you, find out exactly what's on offer before committing yourselves to a firm booking.

Bear in mind that you aren't likely to get much of a feel for 'real life' in a resort of this type. Your neighbours will probably be other foreign visitors, and the Italians running it may well be jaded by too much exposure to tourists. Rents are often high, and the on-site facilities can sometimes be over-priced, leaving you with the sad feeling that you've been fleeced. It's not always easy to check up on things like prices in the 'village' shop before you get there, but you can find out how far you'll be from the nearest town. Then, if you're taking your own car, you can always use the apartment as a base and do your shopping elsewhere.

VILLAS

Villa holidays are usually at the top end of the market. Some companies (see Chapter 3) specialize in renting luxury villas usually equipped with a swimming pool, several bathrooms, comfortable furniture, and a maid to do the cleaning. It is also possible to book a villa on a more modest scale.

Whoever you rent from, the villa is likely to be a beautiful building with a history that may go back to the Middle Ages. In some places, the view alone will be worth paying rent for. Villas are almost always found in a rural setting, and you'll get quite a feel for country life. There may be people working in the fields around the house, and they are often friendly and interested to meet you – especially if you are the only tourist in the area. In fact, if you stay a few weeks, you may even lose the sense of being a tourist and start to feel as if you are part of the local community. You can often buy wine, cheese and vegetables from local farms – another way of getting to meet your neighbours.

Whatever the charms of a holiday in the middle of the country, you'd be wise to think carefully about transport before you book. Buses tend to be rare and erratic in more isolated places, and it's best to have a car. Even so, country roads aren't always made up and, in extreme heat, driving can be arduous. This won't matter if you simply want to stay put. However, if there are children in your party, think long and hard about what they are going to do. It's extremely hot in midsummer – no long country walks during the day. If there's a swimming pool or river you'll be all right, and a short walk to the nearest bar for ice-creams is usually a popular pastime too.

FLATS OR APARTMENTS

Most Italian city dwellers live in flats. These are often situated in part of a huge *palazzo* (palace) that has been divided up and sold off by the original owners. In this case there will be a vast front door and a grand communal staircase. Post is usually sent to a series of named mail boxes in the main hall (see

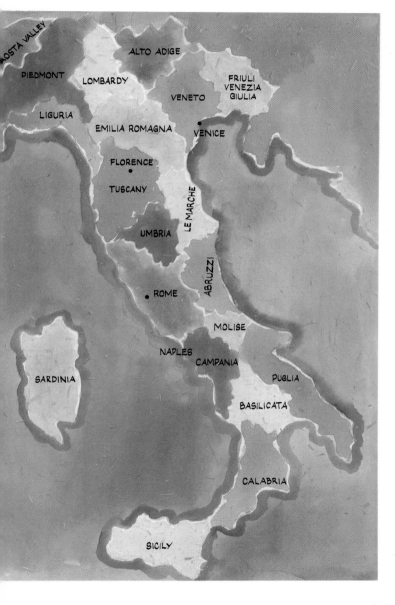

Chapter 12, CONTACT WITH HOME).

Many flats have a small balcony – this is particularly common in modern, purpose-built flats. Even if there's no balcony, you will probably have the right to dry your clothes outside somewhere. The washing line may be suspended high above the street or over an inaccessible internal courtyard – don't drop anything or you'll never see it again.

ISLAND HOLIDAYS

Almost all the islands off the Italian coast now have a tourist trade of some kind or another. However, the standard of accommodation varies enormously. If you are going to one of the remoter islands – particularly in the South – don't expect luxury accommodation. Very often you'll be offered one of the local houses to live in. This is likely to be simple, functional, extremely pretty, but in no way luxurious. The kitchen and bathroom are likely to offer only the bare essentials. But in those wonderful surroundings, who needs more? Water can be scarce on the islands, so don't expect to soak in a deep bath every night.

WHAT ABOUT CHILDREN – AND BABIES?

You'll find that you and your children receive a warm welcome in Italy. It's a child centred society – a holiday in itself for English parents.

When it comes to packing, what you can take will depend very much on how you're going to travel. You'll be able to take a lot more if you're going by car. However, the journey will be longer so you'll need to be prepared to entertain and feed the children as well. If you plan to travel by plane weight restrictions will impose a limit on your packing. Bear in mind that you'll probably have more to carry on the way home. For train travellers weight will again be the main concern – just how much can you manage if there isn't a porter or a trolley at the other end?

If you're travelling with a baby it can be quite helpful to pack a small travelling bag for the journey (see Chapter 4, GETTING READY).

Your main concern should be with taking the right sort of clothes. If you're going in summer, you can keep these to a minimum. In the summer pure cotton is the only suitable fabric for children's clothes – man-made fabrics can become very sticky in real heat. Take garments with long sleeves and legs. This is particularly important if you have a child with fair skin that won't tolerate constant exposure to the sun. Babies and children should all be equipped with wide-brimmed hats. Babies' faces can be burnt by reflected rays even if they are sitting in the shade. The peaked caps sold for little boys in this country won't give enough protection. A detachable sun-shade for the pushchair or a canopy for the pram will also be essential at the height of summer.

Plastic sandals may be useful on the beach when the sand is too hot to walk on, but they will be intolerably hot and sticky under any other circumstances. Feet swell in the heat, so make sure that children's shoes are large enough.

Boots the chemists make a good sun shield that can be stuck onto the car window. If your children are young enough to use car seats, make sure that they have cotton covers – the acrylic ones become very hot and sticky. Take a towel or blanket to cover the buckles when the car seat is empty; if they aren't protected from the sun they can get so hot that you can't use the seat.

Older children will need books and games, tapes and suitable food. Be prepared – after all, the journey is part of the holiday. (See also Chapter 4, GETTING READY.)

Check to see if a cot will be provided if necessary. If not, buy or borrow one and get the child used to it before you leave. Make sure you take cotton sheets for the hot nights – a cotton towel under the sheet will also soak up any sweat and keep the baby comfortable.

When you're on the move you'll find that every effort is made to meet the needs of mothers and children. Even the smaller airports usually have 'mother and baby' rooms, and so do motorway service stations. Train stations aren't quite so reliable.

The shops at the larger motorway service stations stock all the essentials for travelling with children. They have babywipes, nappies, powder, baby food, biscuits, juice, travel games, sweets, tapes and lots more. You'll also be able to eat at the self-service restaurant. This can be a boon with children as they can choose exactly what they want. The food is generally very good – they often include regional specialities (*specialità regionali*), on the menu. If you don't want a full meal the bar will sell sandwiches, filled rolls and other snacks.

Despite the national fondness for children, Italian children's toys aren't usually as good as ours. Don't rely on being able to buy something cheap and cheerful for the children when you get there. Seaside resorts have all the usual buckets and spades but elsewhere it can be difficult to find anything that isn't imported and tremendously expensive.

CHAPTER THREE

MAKING PLANS

Obviously, the two most important things to consider are the property and the travelling. These are dealt with in this chapter, which includes a list of travel companies researched especially for this book.

FINDING A HOUSE OR APARTMENT

You may have a property in mind from the outset – one that has been recommended, for instance, or one that belongs to friends. If not, you have to start hunting.

Generally speaking, the earlier you book the better, as the choice of property for the weeks you want will be wider than if you book at short notice. While it's not out of the question, especially in low season, to turn up somewhere and expect to find a house of the sort you want on the spot, this can be a fairly risky plan of action either if children are involved or if the budget won't stretch to a few nights in a hotel, should they prove necessary.

You may start your search in your local travel agency, but a look through the weekend papers will usually reveal a host of small ads. Some are obviously for companies, others describe a specific property and give the owner's phone number (maybe in the UK, maybe in Italy). Some *appear* to be private, but are actually placed by companies.

PRIVATE ADS

There's much to be said for booking direct with the owners – they should certainly know the property and the area, and be able to give quite detailed advice. If it's a house they use regularly themselves, you can be fairly confident that it will be well equipped (and you can ask them, of course – but see also WHAT TO TAKE in Chapter 4).

Theoretically it should be less expensive to book direct with an owner – but you can only know for sure if you shop around and make a comparison with properties on offer from the travel firms.

Try to see photographs before you book, and ask for the names and phone numbers of a few 'satisfied customers' – the people you are renting from may *sound* wonderful, but you don't know them, after all.

You will probably be asked for a deposit of something like 25–40% of the total rental. Make sure this is all backed up in writing, and be clear about what happens if you need to cancel. It's usual to get a substantial portion of the deposit back if you cancel a couple of months before planned departure, and to forfeit the whole amount if you cancel at the last minute. Remember that travel insurance will often cover cancellation costs, so look into it as soon as you are about to part with any money. The main thing about booking independently like this is that you have to thrash out these details for yourself.

If you book privately, check that the owners have property and contents insurance that covers any damage or breakages you or your party might make, and make sure, too, that their insurance covers you if the roof collapses on one of your party or in case any of you are injured by fire, for instance – unlikely to happen, but it's essential to check.

All of this applies whether the owner is based in Italy, or not. Take into account the cost of international phone calls as you make your arrangements . . .

RENTING FROM FRIENDS

This is likely to be an informal procedure, without any deposits, etc. But check the position on insurance (see PRIVATE ADS, above).

HOME EXCHANGE

Another possibility is house-swopping, which can be arranged through an organization such as Intervac, which aims to promote international friendship. This gives you the opportunity to stay in a genuine Italian house, while the Italians spend their holiday in your home. The benefits are many – not least the fact that there is no rent to pay. Contact Intervac Great Britain, Hazel Nayar, 6 Siddals Lane, Allestree, Derby DE3 2DY; phone 0332 558931.

TRAVEL COMPANIES

Broadly speaking, the companies fall into three categories: first, there are the big travel firms who offer countless sorts of holidays to countless destinations, including self-catering holidays in Italy. They often have huge numbers of properties, and these may be handled on site on their behalf by small, local companies. Brochures from these firms are the ones travel agents are most likely to have, and booking can generally be arranged through a travel agent quite easily, as well as direct with the company.

In the middle come the medium-to-large independent operators who specialize in self-catering, with houses and apartments all over the country (and maybe in other countries too), often with 60 or 70 (though possibly several hundred) properties on their books. They tend to resemble either the big firms or the small specialists, depending on the size of their operation.

At the other end of the scale are the independent firms, often quite tiny, specializing in houses in particular regions. A family team with a dozen houses near to Siena or in the Lakes, say, would be typical. These people are likely to know each house on their list quite well, and might be better than a big company in providing for special requests or needs – if they are given plenty of warning! You generally have to contact these firms direct.

It's impossible to give any hard and fast rules about whether large companies or small ones are likely to be more expensive – our survey of some 65 firms that offer self-catering holidays in Italy showed that the price reflects the location and the luxuriousness of the property rather than company size. Get hold of brochures or information from several firms for the type of property, area and period you want, and make a price comparison yourself.

Most of these companies offer to arrange travel for you. The big firms tend to expect you to arrange your flight through them, so they quote all-in prices. Some companies offer car ferry or motorail as an option, too. Not many offer solely rental. (The specific information on travel comes later, in TRAVEL OPTIONS.)

UK-BASED COMPANIES OFFERING SELF-CATERING HOLIDAYS IN ITALY

We have tried to make this listing as comprehensive and as accurate as possible, and all the information in it was provided by the companies concerned. Please remember that inclusion in the list does not constitute a recommendation, nor are we suggesting that companies *not* included are unreliable.

As well as names and addresses, the listing includes telephone numbers and, in some cases, special phone numbers for ordering brochures – usually they have an answering machine taking brochure requests, which are dealt with very quickly. The directory also includes the regions of Italy where the companies operate, plus a short description of their type of business, and the approximate number of properties on their books.

Many of these companies offer travel as well as accommodation – details are provided in the list. Give travel plenty of thought before booking (the options are discussed later in this chapter).

The listing also includes companies' registration with, or membership of, various bodies – ABTA, ATOL and AITO:

What is ABTA? The Association of British Travel Agents is a self-governing body which aims to ensure high standards of service and business practice from its members.

Tour operators and travel agents can be members of ABTA. Members should display their ABTA Number on all brochures and advertising, and are required to adhere to a code of conduct, drawn up in association with the Office of Fair Trading, concerning brochure descriptions, advertising, booking conditions etc.

Should an ABTA member go out of business, the Association will ensure that customers can continue their holiday as planned and return home, and will repay customers who have paid for holidays which have not yet started. In the event of you being dissatisfied with your holiday, ABTA has a conciliation and arbitration procedure for dealing with complaints.

You may therefore prefer to book your holiday through an ABTA travel agent or tour operator for added protection and peace of mind. For further details contact the Association of British Travel Agents (see USEFUL ADDRESSES at the end of this chapter).

What is ATOL? An Air Tours Operators Licence, ATOL, is issued by the Civil Aviation Authority and is a legal requirement for all tour operators who use charter flights (although it does not apply to scheduled flights).

The scheme provides protection for customers such that if the tour company fails, the CAA will ensure that customers on holiday can finish their trip and travel home as planned, and that people who have paid for a holiday which they have not yet taken will be reimbursed. You should look for the operator's ATOL number on brochures and advertisements to ensure that you qualify for this cover. For more information contact the Civil Aviation Authority (see USEFUL ADDRESSES, at the end of this chapter).

What is AITO? The Association of Independent Tour Operators is an alliance of some 70 small tour companies, all specializing in a particular country or type of holiday. All members are fully bonded, either through ABTA, the Civil Aviation Authority, or by private arrangement with insurance companies or banks, so that your holiday is protected.

AA MOTORING HOLIDAYS
P.O. Box 100, Fanum House,
Halesowen, West Midlands B63 3BT
Phone 021 550 7401
Fax 021 585 5336
Automobile Association's tour operator specializing in self-drive holidays in Europe for members and non-members.
ABTA ATOL

25 properties in Tuscany.
Ferry Motorail

ALLEGRO HOLIDAYS
15a–17a Church Street, Reigate, Surrey RH2 OAA
Phone 0737 221323
Fax 0737 233590
Imaginative, independent company offering flexibility. ABTA ATOL AITO

40 properties in Campania, Umbria, Tuscany, Sicily, Sardinia, Venice.
Flight Car hire Fly/drive

AUTO PLAN HOLIDAYS
Energy House, Lombard Street,
Lichfield, Staffordshire WS15 6DP
Phone 0543 257777
Fax 0543 415469
Family business offering a choice of self-catering holidays in Italy for motorists.

20 properties in Tuscany, Alto Adige, Lake Garda.
Ferry Flight Car hire Fly/drive Motorail

BEACH VILLAS (HOLIDAYS) LIMITED
8 Market Passage, Cambridge CB2 3QR
Phone 0223 311113
Brochure line 0223 350777
Fax 0223 313557

Family business specializing in villas and apartments throughout Europe.
ABTA ATOL

75 properties in Calabria, Tuscany, Elba.
Ferry Flight Car hire Fly/drive Motorail

BELLA TOSCANA (UK) LIMITED
7 Dere Close, Bourne, Lincolnshire PE10 9XQ
Phone 0778 425795
Fax 0778 33282
Family business with personal links with Tuscan owned property. Specialists in stone houses with pools in the Florence area (can assist with travel).

60 properties in Tuscany.

BLAKES VILLAS
Wroxham, Norwich, Norfolk NR12 8DH
Phone 0603 784141
Brochure line 0533 460606
Fax 0603 782871
Long-established company offering self-catering holidays in Umbria and Tuscany. ABTA ATOL

74 properties in Umbria, Tuscany.
Ferry Fly/drive Motorail

BOWHILLS
Mayhill Farm, Mayhill Lane,
Swanmore, Southampton, Hampshire SO3 2QW
Phone 0489 877627
Brochure line 0489 878567
Fax 0489 877872
Family run company with over 17 years' experience offering a range of properties in good positions, most with pools.
ATOL

45 properties in Umbria, Tuscany.
Ferry Flight Car hire Fly/drive Motorail

BRIDGEWATER VILLAS
37 King Street West, Manchester
M3 2PW
Phone 061 834 6464
Brochure line 061 832 6011
Fax 061 832 6020

Independent family business with offices in Italy specializing in tailormade self-catering holidays. ABTA

200 properties in Umbria, Tuscany, Alto Adige, Aosta Valley, Florence, Colle Val d'Elsa.

Car hire Fly/drive Motorail

CITALIA CIT (England) LIMITED
Marco Polo House, 3–5 Lansdowne Road, Croydon, Surrey CR9 1LL
Phone 081 686 0677
Fax 081 686 0328

Tour operator offering a large range of self-catering holidays in Italy. ABTA ATOL AITO

Apulia, Campania, Umbria, Tuscany, Emilia Romagna, Liguria, Veneto, Sicily, Sardinia, Florence, Venice.

Ferry Flight Car hire Fly/drive Motorail Train/car hire

CONTINENTAL VILLAS
Eagle House, 58 Blythe Road, London W14 0HA
Phone 071 371 1313
Fax 071 602 4165

Independent tour operator specializing in the luxury end of the market.

350 properties in Umbria, Tuscany, Veneto, Florence, Venice.

Ferry Flight Car hire Fly/drive Motorail Train/car hire

COSTA SMERALDA HOLIDAYS
140 Walton Street, London SW3 2JJ
Phone 071 493 8303
Fax 071 581 2397

Small company specializing in luxury villas in Sardinia. ATOL

20 properties in Sardinia.

Flight

CV TRAVEL
43 Cadogan Street, London SW3 2PR
Phone 071 581 0851
Brochure line 071 589 0132
Fax 071 584 5229

Family business specializing in self-catering accommodation in unspoilt locations in Italy. ABTA ATOL AITO

35 properties in Campania, Umbria, Tuscany.

Flight Car hire Fly/drive

DAVID NEWMAN'S EUROPEAN COLLECTION
P.O. Box 733, 40 Upperton Road, Eastbourne, Sussex BN21 4AW
Phone 0323 410347
Fax 0323 410347

A family business offering flexibility and attention to detail. ABTA

1000 properties in Tuscany, Florence.

Ferry

ERNA LOW CONSULTANTS
9 Reece Mews, London SW7 3HE
Phone 071 584 2841
Brochure line 071 584 7820

Small company offering a consultancy, a representation service, and a sales department. Specialists in sports and health holidays.

Tuscany, Veneto, Alto Adige, Aosta Valley, Sicily, Florence.

Ferry Flight Car hire Fly/drive Motorail Train/car hire

EUROVILLAS (1967) LIMITED
36 East Street, Coggeshall, Essex CO6 1SH
Phone 0376 561156

Small family business offering self-catering holidays in the less commercialized areas of Italy.

Tuscany, Alto Adige, Piedmont, Lucca.

Ferry Flight Car hire Fly/drive Motorail

FALCON SAILING LIMITED
Hillgate House, 13 Hillgate Street, London W8 7SP
Phone 071 727 0232
Fax 071 792 3142

Specialist watersports operator.
Properties at the company's dinghy
sailing and windsurfing centre in
Sardinia. ABTA ATOL

5 properties in Sardinia.

GORDON OVERLAND
76 Croft Road, Carlisle, Cumbria
CH3 9AG
Phone 0228 26795
Fax 0228 26795

Travel consultancy specializing in villa
rental and group and individual tours
throughout Europe.

200 properties in Umbria, Tuscany,
Rome, Florence, Venice, Siena.

Ferry Flight Car hire

**HARRISON-STANTON AND
HASLAM LIMITED**
25 Studdridge Street, London SW6 3SL
Phone 071 736 5094
Fax 071 384 2327

Small business specializing in
beautifully restored properties
including a 12th-century castle) in
Tuscany and Umbria – most with pools.

0 properties in Umbria, Tuscany.

Motorail

**HOSEASONS HOLIDAYS ABROAD
LIMITED**
Sunway House, Lowestoft, Suffolk
NR32 3LT
Phone 0502 500555
Brochure line 0502 501501
Fax 0502 500532

Self-catering specialists with over 45
years' experience offering a small
programme of quality accommodation in
Tuscany. ABTA ATOL

0 properties in Umbria, Tuscany,
Veneto, Venice.

Ferry Flight Car hire Fly/drive Motorail
Train/car hire

INTASUN HOLIDAYS
Intasun House, Cromwell Avenue,
Bromley, Kent BR2 9AQ
Phone 081 290 0511
Fax 081 466 4406

Major tour operator offering a range of
travel inclusive self-catering holidays
throughout Europe. ABTA ATOL

13 properties in Calabria.

Flight Car hire

INTERHOME
383 Richmond Road, Twickenham,
Middlesex TW1 2EF
Phone 081 891 1924
Fax 081 891 5331

Largest holiday accommodation agency
in Europe offering all standards of
property including chalets, villas and
apartments.

Properties in Calabria, Basilicata,
Campania, Umbria, Tuscany, Liguria,
Veneto, Alto Adige, Lombardy, Aosta
Valley, Sicily, Sardinia, Rome,
Florence, Venice.

Ferry Motorail

INTERMEZZO ITALIA
10 Barley Mow Passage, London
W4 4PH
Phone 081 994 6477
Brochure line 081 993 1752
Fax 081 995 0828

Specialists in 'Agritourism', they offer a
wide range of villas and apartments in
classical settings, many with pools.
ATOL

80 properties in Lazio, Umbria, Le
Marche, Tuscany, Liguria, Lombardy,
Rome, Florence, Venice.

Ferry Flight Car hire Motorail

INTERNATIONAL CHAPTERS
126 St John's Wood Terrace, London
NW8 6PL
Phone 071 722 9560
Fax 071 722 9140

Privately owned company offering a
large choice of properties ranging from
castles to farmhouses and apartments.
ABTA AITO

1500 properties in Umbria, Le Marche,
Tuscany, Veneto, Sicily, Rome,
Florence, Venice, Lucca, Siena, San
Gimingano.

Ferry Flight Car hire Fly/drive Motorail

INVITATION TO TUSCANY
78 Selwyn Road, Edgbaston,
Birmingham B16 0SW
Phone 021 454 3322
Fax 021 454 3322

Specialists in the Florence/Siena area,
offering farmhouses, villas and
apartments, some with pools.

45 properties in Tuscany, Florence,
Siena.

Ferry Car hire

ITALIA NEL MONDO TRAVEL SERVICES LIMITED
6 Palace Street, London SW1E 5HY
Phone 071 828 9171
Fax 071 630 5184

Small company specializing in
self-catering holidays in Sicily and the
Eolian Islands. ATOL

40 properties in Tuscany, Sicily and the
Eolian Islands, Florence.

Flight Car hire Fly/drive

ITALIAN ESCAPADES
227 Shepherds Bush Road, London
W6 7AS
Phone 081 748 4999
Brochure line 081 563 0379
Fax 081 748 6381

Branch of a major tour operator
specializing in 'design your own
holiday'. It is possible to combine self-
catering with city breaks in hotels.
ABTA ATOL

20 properties in Umbria, Tuscany,
Emilia Romagna, Veneto, Sardinia.

Flight Car hire Fly/drive Train/car hire

ITALIAN INTERLUDE
91 Regent Street, London W1R 7TB
Phone 071 494 2031
Fax 071 287 2142

Medium sized company specializing
mainly in family self-catering holidays.
ABTA ATOL

200 properties in Campania, Lazio,
Umbria, Tuscany, Veneto, Lombardy,
Sardinia.

Flight Car hire Fly/drive

JUST ITALY
1 Belmont, Lansdown Road, Bath
BA1 5DZ
Phone 0225 443133
Brochure line 0225 448894
Fax 0225 444520

Company offering a selection of villas,
country houses and apartments in Italy.
ABTA ATOL AITO

40 properties in Umbria, Tuscany,
Island of Elba.

Ferry Fly/drive Motorail

LUNIGIANA HOLIDAYS
71 Busbridge Lane, Godalming, Surrey
GU7 1QQ
Phone 04868 21218
Fax 04868 23882

Family business specializing in houses
in Tuscany.

40 properties in Tuscany, Liguria,
Florence.

Ferry Flight Car hire Motorail

MAGIC OF ITALY
227 Shepherds Bush Road, London
W6 7AS
Phone 081 748 7575
Brochure line 081 741 1349
Fax 081 563 0480

Medium sized company offering villas
and apartments, many with pools,
throughout Italy. Specialists in
self-catering holidays for two
passengers. ABTA ATOL AITO

30 properties in Campania, Umbria,
Tuscany, Lombardy, Sicily, Sardinia,
Florence, Venice, Verona.

Ferry Flight Car hire Fly/drive

MEON VILLA HOLIDAYS
Meon House, College Street,
Petersfield, Hampshire GU32 3JN
Phone 0730 66561
Fax 0730 68482

Medium sized company offering a
selection of self-catering holidays in
villas (with private or shared pools) and
apartments. ABTA ATOL

50 properties in Umbria, Tuscany.

Ferry Flight Car hire

OSL
4 Broadway, Edgbaston Five Ways,
Birmingham B15 1BB
Phone 021 643 2727
Brochure line 021 632 6282
Fax 021 643 7267

Medium sized company specializing in
villas, farmhouses and apartments,
mostly with pools. Car-hire is included
in the price of every holiday. ABTA
50 properties in Tuscany.
Flight Car hire

PEGASUS HOLIDAYS
River House, Restmor Way,
Hackbridge Road, Wallington, Surrey
SM6 7AH
Phone 081 773 2442
Fax 081 773 2132

Specialist Italian company offering a
wide range of properties, some with
pools. ABTA ATOL
10 properties in Umbria, Le Marche,
Tuscany, Emilia Romagna.
Ferry Flight Car hire Fly/drive

SALLY HOLIDAYS
1 Piccadilly, London W1V 9HF
Phone 071 355 2266
Fax 071 355 3008

Tour operator arm of ferry company
Sally Line. Specialists in self-drive
holidays to Europe. ABTA ATOL
10 properties in Tuscany,
Lombardy, Alto Adige.
Ferry

FV HOLIDAYS LIMITED
Summer House, Hernes Road,
Summertown, Oxford OX2 7PU
Phone 0865 577381
Brochure line 0865 311331
Fax 0865 310682

Large tour operator offering a range of
travel inclusive self-catering holidays in
Tuscany. ATOL
10 properties in Tuscany, Florence.
Ferry Flight Car hire Fly/drive Motorail
Train/car hire

THE TRAVEL CLUB OF
UPMINSTER
Station Road, Upminster, Essex
RM14 2TT
Phone 04022 25000
Fax 04022 29678

Direct sell tour operator offering all-
inclusive holidays to the Italian Lakes.
ABTA ATOL
1 property in Lombardy.
Flight

TRADITIONAL TUSCANY
108 Westcombe Park Road, Blackheath,
London SE3 7RZ
Phone 081 305 1380

Family business offering authentic
country houses and cottages in the
Tuscan countryside.
24 properties in Umbria, Tuscany,
Florence.

TUSCANY FROM COTTAGES TO
CASTLES
Tuscany House, 351 Tonbridge Road,
Maidstone, Kent ME16 8NH
Phone 0622 726883
Fax 0622 729835

Medium sized tour operator specializing
in self-catering holidays in Umbria and
Tuscany.
344 properties in Umbria, Tuscany,
Florence, Siena.
Ferry Flight Car hire Fly/drive Motorail

VACANZE IN ITALIA
Bignor, Nr. Pulborough, West Sussex
RH20 1QD
Phone 0798 7426
Brochure line 0798 7421
Fax 0798 7343

Specialists in self-catering holidays in
Italy, offering properties throughout the
country, many with pools. ATOL
200 properties in Apulia, Umbria,
Tuscany, Rome, Florence, Venice.
Ferry Flight Car hire Fly/drive Motorail

VERONICA TOMASSO COTGROVE
10 St Mark's Crescent, London
NW1 7TS
Phone 071 267 2423
Fax 071 485 1480

Family business specializing in houses in Tuscany and Umbria. Culture holidays also available.

25 properties in Umbria, Tuscany, Rome, Lucca, Pisa.

VILLA ALTERNATIVES
17 Montpelier Street, London
SW7 1HG
Phone 071 584 1030
Brochure line 081 780 2899

Tailor made villa rental service. All properties have pool and staff, sleeping from 6 to 16 people. ABTA ATOL AITO

Umbria, Tuscany, Lombardy, Sardinia.
Ferry Flight Car hire

VILLAS IN EUROPE
53 St Owen Street, Hereford HR1 2JQ
Phone 0432 263333
Fax 0432 58393

Villa specialists offering a wide range of properties in conjunction with a long established Florentine self-catering company. ABTA

310 properties in Umbria, Tuscany, Florence.

Ferry Flight Car hire Fly/drive Motorail Train/car hire

VILLAS ITALIA
Hillgate House, 13 Hillgate Street, London W8 7SP
Phone 071 221 4432
Fax 071 792 3146

Small up-market Italy specialist offering villas and apartments throughout Italy, specializing in the Tuscany area. ABTA ATOL

150 properties in Campania, Umbria, Tuscany, Liguria, Sardinia, Florence, Venice.

Ferry Flight Car hire Fly/drive

WORLD WINE TOURS
4 Dorchester Road, Drayton St Leonard, Oxfordshire 0X10 7BH
Phone 0865 891919
Fax 0865 891337

Specialist tour operator arranging travel into fine wine regions. Self-catering holidays offered at a leading wine estate between Florence and Siena.

1 property in Tuscany.
Flight Car hire Fly/drive

THE TRAVEL OPTIONS

Travelling to Italy from the UK, the main options are: *fly/drive* (i.e. with a hire car waiting at your destination); *fligh only*; *taking your car* – using ferry or hovercraft and drivin through France, or through Germany if you are coming fron the North; *taking your car and using motorail* (including a ferr crossing); *train* (with ferry crossing); *train plus car hire* (wit ferry crossing).

As you decide how you want to travel, weigh u comfort/speed/stress etc. against cost. The main points to tak into consideration are:

- whether you want to treat the journey as part of the holiday or as a necessary evil
- how much holiday you have and how long you are prepared to spend travelling
- how far you live from the main ferry ports, and how far into Italy your destination lies
- how far you live from an airport
- how far you are prepared to drive
- the number of people who can share driving
- the timing: if you're thinking of driving through France, remember that the French roads are packed on the first and last weekends of August, and during the weekend of their 15 August public holiday
- whether you want/can afford to make overnight stops
- the size of the party (a full carload costs much the same to transport as a half-empty one)
- whether your party minds long sea crossings or flying
- whether flights are available in your budget range
- how unrestricted you want your luggage to be (do you need a carload of baby things, or want to take the windsurfer?)

TAKING YOUR CAR – DISTANCE, ROUTE AND ATTITUDE

If you decide to drive, there are two approaches you can take – the dawdler or a dasher. Dawdlers make the journey a part of the holiday, acknowledging that there's plenty to see *en route* to or from their main holiday place. Dashers pile into the car and *drive*. It's quite common for members of a party to have differing attitudes to the drive, some being by nature dawdlers, while others are dashers, so compromises often have to be made. You could always dash one way and dawdle the other.

If you live in the Midlands or South, it's quite straight-forward and quick to get to a Channel port and hop over to France. Crossings from the south-east corner of England (Dover, Ramsgate, etc.) are plentiful and fast (details of ferries appear below).

From the North, North Wales or Scotland there's a long and exhausting drive to the Channel ports, before the drive on the other side of the Channel even starts. And while the prospect of a long drive may not sound too bad when there's a two-week holiday in which to get over it, think of the return journey . . . back late on Sunday and back to the old routine next day, probably.

At some stage, regardless of how many drivers you have, it's a good idea to stop for a rest and sleep. The most pleasant way is a relaxed stop at a small hotel with good dinner and a comfortable bed.

Dashing through France, you will inevitably use the *autoroutes*. Most of France's motorways are toll roads (*autoroutes à péage*). Prices per kilometre vary, and travelling from, for example, Calais to the Alps will cost around £30. This will be in addition to the cost of petrol. (Prices are per vehicle, irrespective of the number of passengers.)

MOTORAIL

The idea of Motorail is that you and your car make a substantial part of your journey by train. British Rail offer the service within Britain, while French Railways (SNCF) offer over 50 services from Paris and the north coast ports to destinations in southern France and Italy.

The main advantage of Motorail is that it takes a lot of the hassle out of long journeys on the continent with a car. You avoid long drives and traffic congestion and should arrive at your destination on time and relaxed. You also save on the petrol, motorway tolls and overnight stop expenses that accumulate on a long drive through France.

Motorail journeys are timed to take place overnight. No conventional accommodation is provided, so you pay for either a *couchette* or a sleeper compartment (*wagon-lits*). A *couchette* is a berth in a compartment – usually there are six people (in triple bunks that fold up to provide seating by day) in each, and you are supplied with a blanket and fresh linen. The compartment may be shared with other travellers

(although a large enough party ought to get one to themselves) and is not segregated according to sex, so it's not normal to undress in a *couchette* compartment. (Having said that, it's best just to use your own discretion – a T-shirt and shorts is quite normal.) *Wagons-lits* are more expensive. They are less cramped, though, and many have washing facilities and you are guaranteed privacy. Many people sleep very well on trains and think this is a terrific way to travel. Light sleepers can find the whole thing miserable and exhausting – you can only know once you've tried it.

On some routes a buffet service is available, but it is advisable to check this before travelling. On all services a free continental breakfast is provided on arrival at your destination while your car is being unloaded. If you are booking your house through a travel company, you may find they will arrange Motorail for you (see the list above). Motorail can be booked directly with SNCF (they have a London office) through P&O European Ferries and through Sealink (see USEFUL ADDRESSES at the end of this chapter). On some services there are special ferry prices for Motorail passengers. See the section below on going by TRAIN.

FERRY SERVICES

FERRY SHIPS

Ships can be good fun on hot summer days when the decks are pleasant to sit out on or stroll around. Inside, the facilities and catering seem to vary enormously not only from one shipping line to another, but from ship to ship.

If you have a vehicle, once you've been waved up the ramp and have parked to the satisfaction of the loading staff, you have to get out of the car fairly quickly and go up to the passenger lounges by the nearest staircase. Remember the name or number of the staircase and your deck number, so you can find your car later! You have to take up with you to the passenger decks anything that you might need during the journey, as you are not allowed back down to your vehicle until the ship docks at the other side. With so many sets of identical-looking stairs it's easy to lose your bearings, so try to hang on to excited children (especially just after embarkation or before disembarkation, when everybody is milling around, and it's easy to become separated).

On short crossings there tends to be something of a stampede as people board and grab sets of seats or tables for their parties. On longer ones it is often necessary to reserve seating when you book. (This applies particularly at night.) Night-time accommodation usually consists of reclining chairs or cabins. Cabins tend to cost something like £20 for a couple, but each ship usually has a few 'luxury' ones at higher prices, that need to be booked well in advance. Standard cabins, usually well below the waterline, are small (as are the bunks), can be poorly ventilated, and tend to pulsate with the throb of the ship's engines. Once you've got used to them, however, you can get a reasonable night's sleep. Many people bed down for the night in a corner of one of the main lounges, and it's quite a good idea to settle children with a couple of blankets. If you want a cabin and haven't booked one, you can ask the purser as you board. (A cabin may be a good idea during the day if everyone is tired, and as they are less in demand you may get a quite pleasant one.)

Facilities on board vary according to the length of the voyage, but there's always food, some sort of duty-free shop, and money-changing facilities. Sometimes there are telephones. TV lounges are quite common, and on longer journeys you may find there's a small cinema on board. Some areas are no smoking.

Not all the ferries are ships, of course:

HOVERCRAFT

On several of the short routes (such as Dover–Calais) hovercraft cross the Channel in about 40–45 minutes. They carry cars, as well as passengers. They tend to be fairly noisy, and to vibrate quite a lot – and even if you get a window seat the view is usually obliterated by spray. However, they halve the journey time (although you take just as long over check-in and customs clearance as in a ferry ship). Refreshments are usually offered (payment required) and a selection of duty-free goods is brought round.

SEACAT

These Australian vessels were introduced by Hoverspeed in summer 1990. They are rather exciting high-speed ferries that cut the crossing time from Portsmouth to Cherbourg by nearly half. They take cars.

The list below shows the ferry routes, the companies and the journey times. Actual departure times are not included as they vary from season to season. [S] Summer sailings only, [C] Seacat. Hovercraft are operated by Hoverspeed.

For further information contact the ferry companies (see USEFUL ADDRESSES at the end of this chapter).

From	To	Company	Duration (hours.min)
TO FRANCE			
Cork	Roscoff	Brittany Ferries	15
Dover	Boulogne	Hoverspeed	.45
Dover	Boulogne	P&O European Ferries	1.40
Dover	Calais	Hoverspeed	.45
Dover	Calais	P&O European Ferries	1.15
Dover	Calais	Sealink	1.30
Folkestone	Boulogne	Sealink	1.50
Newhaven	Dieppe	Sealink	4
Ramsgate	Dunkirk	Sally Lines	2.30
Rosslare	Cherbourg	Irish Ferries	17
Rosslare	Le Havre	Irish Ferries	23
Plymouth	Roscoff	Brittany Ferries	7
Poole	Cherbourg	Brittany Ferries	4.15 [S]

Portsmouth	Caen	Brittany Ferries	6
Portsmouth	Cherbourg	P&O European Ferries	4.45 [S]
Portsmouth	Cherbourg	Hoverspeed	2.40 [C]
Portsmouth	Le Havre	P&O European Ferries	5.45
Portsmouth	St Malo	Brittany Ferries	9

Depending on your starting point and destination, these may be useful too:

TO BELGIUM

| Felixstowe | Zeebrugge | P&O European Ferries | 5.45 |
| Hull | Zeebrugge | North Sea Ferries | 14.30 |

TO HOLLAND

| Hull | Rotterdam | North Sea Ferries | 14 |
| Sheerness | Vlissingen | Olau Line | 8 |

TRAIN

If you are not taking a car, and do not like flying, train travel could provide a good solution – but an expensive one. You could hire a car to use at your destination (see HIRING A CAR, this chapter). There's no reason why you shouldn't drive or take the train to any Channel port, cross as foot passengers and then take the train from the French Channel port, possibly picking up a hire car at the station at the end of your rail journey.

This sort of arrangement might need careful planning to make sure it worked financially, as a return train trip from London to central Italy via Dover–Calais and France is around £150 per adult. (There are reductions for children and young people, depending on their age.)

Though long-distance rail travel through France is now extremely fast, thanks to their high-speed TGV (*Trains à grande vitesse*) network, the international trains are not TGV.

You would have to make several changes and pay extra to use the TGV, which would hardly be worthwhile.

Some tour companies (see the listing) arrange rail travel or rail travel and car hire. But it's very easy to arrange this yourself. British Rail International (Victoria Station, London – see USEFUL ADDRESSES at the end of this chapter) can arrange ferry or hovercraft plus train to anywhere in Italy starting either in London or at a port. They also have a credit card booking service, so you can book and pay for international tickets over the phone, and simply pick them up on your way. Your own railway station may be able to arrange tickets for you, or advise.

FLIGHTS

Although normal tickets on scheduled flights (allowing you to change departure dates and times after booking) are expensive, there are much better deals available if you book well in advance, or spend at least one Saturday night away, or plan to be away for at least a month. (In each of these cases you have to fix dates and times when you book, and they cannot be changed later.) Airlines such as British Airways or Alitalia are the obvious ones to ask, but you might find that a less well known operator offers flights from your local airport to one close to your destination. You can ask a travel agent or simply ring the airport. Flights can be booked through an agent or direct with the airline. You can sometimes do it over the phone if you have a credit card.

The other sort of flights are the charters, and Italy is one of the biggest charter destinations. At their simplest, they work as follows: big tour companies charter a plane able to take, say, 150 passengers from Birmingham to Milan each Saturday through the summer, and to bring 150 back. However, it could be the case that they end up with less than 150 holidaymakers, so they sell flight-only deals to independent travellers to fill up the seats. Travel agents can usually find out about this and make bookings for you.

As a very rough guide, a standard air fare to a Italian city might cost about £180 return; a non-transferable one booked in advance may be £95 or so; while a charter could be anything between £65 and £85.

Scheduled flights do have some advantages: they seem to fare better than charters on those busy summer days when air traffic congestion causes hold-ups. They may depart and arrive at more sociable hours than charters. Remember that a 4 a.m. departure might mean a night in a hotel, or a special taxi ride – balance that against the possible extra expense of a scheduled flight.

Very cheap deals can sometimes be found in the back of the Sunday newspapers, from travel agents who sell tickets bought in bulk. While these may be tempting, it is advisable to check the details fully before sending any money, although they are probably quite above board.

It is very risky to rely on getting cheap, last-minute, flights if you have already booked your accommodation for specific dates.

Travelling by air, you always have to pay for children, and usually for even quite tiny ones. However, this varies from airline to airline, so do check. Get an assurance, too, that the child gets a seat and does not have to sit on your lap. People with babies in carrycots are usually put in the seats with plenty of leg-room – but do ask. And find out whether you can make a seat reservation as you book – this varies from airline to airline, too, and can depend on the type of ticket you have. Generally speaking, the assistance and facilities are better when planes are not too crowded, and worse on a full flight.

Baggage is restricted on planes. It's usually 20kg (about 40lbs) which is more than most people can carry comfortably. If you are worried about exceeding your allowance you're probably packing too much. Uncrowded flights are much less strict about allowances than full ones.

Take into account the hidden costs and the total journey time: investigate the practicalities of a 5.30 a.m. departure before you pay for it. Watch out, too, for the departure time at the other end – will you need a night in a hotel on your way back? It's worth looking into the expense of railway, taxi or car-parking. Don't ever park in the airport short-stay car park unless you're just dropping people off or picking them up – a fortnight in there would cost almost as much as your holiday. As far as time goes, although the flight itself may be a mere hour and a half, add up the time getting from home to the airport, hanging round at the airport, etc.

HIRING A CAR

If you wish to hire a car for your holiday it is a good idea to arrange this from home before you go as this is likely to be considerably cheaper than arranging it upon arrival in Italy. You can also be more sure about the terms and conditions of the rental agreement.

You may find that the company through which you book your accommodation also offers car hire. Alternatively, the large car-hire companies, as well as many other travel agents and tour operators, offer car hire abroad. It is advisable to shop around the different companies for the best deal as many of these firms offer special deals for holidaymakers inclusive of local tax and insurance.

Be sure to specify special needs, such as child seats, when you arrange the hire, rather than when you arrive at your destination.

If you do decide to arrange to hire a car when you get there, things are a bit more complicated. Check the terms of the rental very carefully. If it is not based on unlimited mileage, make sure that the car's current mileage is recorded on the booking form. You should also ensure that any damage to the vehicle is recorded, that you are fully insured, and that the car contains all the necessary equipment (see TAKING YOUR CAR – THE PRACTICALITIES in Chapter 4).

MOUNTAIN PASSES

If you drive to Italy you are certain to use mountain passes. These are usually quite exciting, and most of the passes provide excellent views of the surrounding area, but many are on narrow roads and often have some tight, unguarded, bends (caravans and trailers are sometimes prohibited).

When planning your route it is a good idea to check the details of passes that you will use (Michelin maps are useful for this). Some smaller ones are closed at night, and many are only open from mid June to September. Tolls are payable on some passes. For further details contact the tourist office or a motoring organization.

TUNNELS

An alternative to passes on some mountain ranges are tunnels. Again, it's best to check the details of tunnels you might use when you plan your route. They vary in length, some being as long as 15 km (9 miles). The quality can vary, too – some are beautifully lit motorway-style tunnels, while others are still rough-hewn from the rock with dodgy lighting. Tolls may be payable, and vary considerably.

Be careful to note any special driving regulations concerning, for example, speed limits and the use of sidelights. And if you're driving by day, remember to turn on your lights as you enter and turn them off after you emerge! If you're wearing light-sensitive sunglasses, they can take some time to adjust to the rapid change of light.

USEFUL ADDRESSES

Name	Address	Tel
Alitalia Italian Airlines	205 Holland Park Avenue London W11	071 602 7111
Association of British Travel Agents	55–57 Newman Street London W1	071 637 2444
Association of Independent Tour Operators	P.O. Box 180 Isleworth Middlesex TW6 7EA	081 569 8092

Automobile Association	Fanum House Basingstoke Hampshire RG21 2EA	0256 20123
British Airways	Heathrow Airport London TW6 2JA	081 759 5511
British Consul (Rome)	British Embassy Via XX Settembre 80A I-00187 Rome	06 4755441
British Motorcyclists Federation	Jack Wiley House 129 Seaforth Avenue Motspur Park Surrey KT3 6JU	081 942 7914
Brittany Ferries	Reservations Offices The Brittany Centre Wharf Road Portsmouth PL1 3EW	0705 827701
British Rail International	Victoria Station London SW1V 1JY	071 834 2345
Civil Aviation Authority	ATOL Section CAA House 45–59 Kingsway London WC2B 6TE	071 832 5620
French Railways (SNCF)	179 Piccadilly London W1	071 409 3518
Irish Ferries Limited	2/4 Miriam Row Dublin 2 Ireland	0001 610511
Italian Consulate-General	38 Eaton Place London SW1 8AN	071 235 9371
Italian State Tourist Board	1 Princes Street London W1R 8AY	071 408 1254
North Sea Ferries	King George Dock Hedon Road Hull North Humberside HU9 5QA	0482 795141

Olau Line Limited	Sheerness Kent ME12 1SN	0795 580010
P&O European Ferries	Dover Kent	0304 203388
Royal Automobile Club	130 St Albans Road Watford WD2 4AH	0923 33543
Royal Yachting Association	RYA House Romsey Road Eastleigh Hampshire SO5 4YA	0703 629962
Sally Ferries	The Argyll Centre York Street Ramsgate Kent CT11 9DS	0843 595522
Sealink UK Limited	Travel Centre Victoria Station London SW1V 1JT	071 828 1940
Thomas Cook Travel (enquiries)	5–7 Priestgate House Priestgate Peterborough PE1 1JF	081 889 7777

CHAPTER FOUR

GETTING READY

THINGS TO ORGANIZE

PASSPORTS

Check that passports are valid for the duration of your holiday. Once they are 16, children need their own passport; before then they can be included on one or both parents' passports (on both is best, just in case one of you needs to come home urgently, for instance).

The standard, 10-year passport, valid worldwide, costs £15. You can obtain application forms from main post offices; the form has to be countersigned by someone who has known you for two years. You need two photographs, as well. You send it to your nearest passport office. *Arrange passports early* - they can take ages, especially during the summer months.

A British Visitor's Passport costs £7.50. It is only valid for one year, so is an expensive option. Also, it is only valid for travel in western Europe (this may have been revised by the time you read this).

INSURANCE

You are strongly advised to take out travel insurance before you go abroad. Holiday insurance will generally cover the following: loss or damage to baggage, loss of money, personal liability, personal accident, departure delay, cancellation or curtailment, legal expenses and medical expenses (including return home in an emergency).

A particularly useful feature of some policies is a 24-hour English-speaking helpline which can be contacted to organize emergency assistance for you.

If you're using a credit card to pay for your holiday you may be able to benefit from free travel insurance which is now offered by some credit and charge card companies. (Check with the company.)

If you book your self-catering accommodation through a UK company, they will probably offer travel insurance. Otherwise it can easily be arranged through travel agents, ferry companies, banks, motoring organizations and insurance brokers and costs around £20 per person for a two-week holiday (with a 50% reduction for children). You can usually organize it on the spot.

Whatever the policy, make sure that it is adequate – at least £100,000 of medical cover in Europe, plus related expenses such as emergency dental treatment, ambulances and if necessary the cost of returning to the UK. Look out for exclusion clauses. For instance, some policies will not cover you if you are driving, pregnant or over 70 years of age; and check whether the clause about 'pre-existing illness or defects' might apply to you. If you're planning to go hang-gliding rock climbing or motorcycle riding check that you'll still be covered in the event of an accident.

Remember that in almost all cases where medical treatment is concerned, you will have to pay up front and reclaim costs from the insurance company. The same goes for car repairs or any other expenses, so keep all receipts. Where theft or loss is concerned, you always have to make a police report (or report to the airline if that's where the problem occurs) Ensure that you keep a copy of it for your insurance company. Generally you have to bear a proportion of the cost yourself – such as the first £15–£20 of each claim. More information in Chapter 12, EMERGENCIES.

FREE HEALTH CARE WITHIN THE EC – FORM E111

Within the European Community a reciprocal agreement allows people from EC countries *some* free medical treatment when they are in other member countries. For UK citizens this procedure is carried out via Form E111.

Getting the E111

Obtaining the E111 is now much less complicated than it used to be. Simply go to any post office (main post offices will be more likely to have them in stock than sub-post offices) and ask for the form. Fill it in and present it to the clerk together with some proof of your British citizenship, such as passport or NHS medical card – a driving licence may be acceptable. The clerk will then stamp the E111 and it will become valid immediately. You will need one for each adult in the party, but children under 16 get registered on a parent's form. Photocopies of the E111 should be accepted abroad, as well as the original.

What the E111 entitles you to

This arrangement entitles you to just the same healthcare that an Italian would be given – but this does not include flying you home or other special treatment. However, it *does* include pre-existing defects, pregnancy-related illness, sporting accidents, and more, which makes it a very useful supplement to travel insurance. The E111 is best thought of as a supplement in Italy.

If you are going to need treatment, you should take the E111 to the Local Health Unit (the USL, or *Unità Sanitaria Locale*). They will exchange it for a certificate of entitlement. Ask them for a list of the scheme's doctors and dentists. When you visit the doctor or dentist you will be treated free of charge if you have the certificate with you – though some special tests may be charged. Without a certificate, you will have to pay up – and it might be difficult to get a refund. Make sure you keep all receipts and price tags for medicines. You will have to pay something for medicines.

The certificate entitles you to treatment at some hospitals, too. If you don't have the certificate in time, show your E111 at the hospital. It is almost certainly best to have other travel insurance, however, rather than rely on this.

INSURANCE FOR DRIVERS/CARS

In addition to personal and medical insurance, those driving abroad should take out adequate insurance to cover breakdown and recovery services when on the continent (see TAKING YOUR CAR, later in this chapter).

TRAVEL

Double check bookings for accommodation, flights, ferries trains, car-hire etc and make sure you have the correct times and dates. Check what is included in the price of the accommodation and confirm any requests for extra beds etc Any tickets or other travel documents should arrive a couple of weeks before you go.

Plan your route if you're driving and allow plenty of time to reach the port or train station if you have ferries and/or motorail booked. Ensure that you have all the necessary equipment and documentation for each country you'll be driving in (see TAKING YOUR CAR – THE PRACTIC ALITIES, later in this chapter).

or. . .

Plan your trip to the airport If you're on a very early flight and live some distance from the airport you might prefer to stay somewhere nearby the night before. For those leaving their car at the airport, make sure you park in the right car park (the long rather than the short-stay one!)

Plan your trip from the airport to your accommodation, don' leave it to chance or you may be stranded!

Find out any luggage restrictions and pack accordingly.

Make a list of emergency phone numbers you might need while away and write an itinerary, together with dates and addresses/telephone numbers, to leave with a close friend o relative.

HOLIDAY MONEY

CURRENCY

The monetary unit is the *lira* (plural *lire*). Notes are issued for 1000, 2000, 5000, 10,000, 20,000, 50,000 and 100,000 lire. £1 = approx 2,300 lire. Coins are 5, 10, 20, 50, 100, 200 and 500 lire. For banking hours, see LOCAL SERVICES in Chapter 11.

There are no restrictions on the amount of money you can take into Italy, but if you intend to export more than 5,000,000 lire at the end of your visit, you should fill in Form V2 at the customs on entry. Otherwise, it's a good idea to change any lire you have left at the end of your holiday in Italy itself, where the rate of exchange is usually better than in the UK.

You will probably want to take money in several forms. Traditionally, travellers cheques have been the most popular way to carry funds on holiday, but use of credit cards and Eurocheques is now very easy, except in the most rural areas. So you can draw on your current account at home, or use a credit card, as easily in Bologna as in Brighton (with travellers cheques, however, you are at least aware of the allocated funds being used up as each one leaves the wallet).

The main points of the most popular alternatives are covered below:

CASH

Changing some money into foreign currency before you go will mean you won't have to search for a bank as soon as you arrive or resort to the poor rates and hefty commission charges of exchanges which operate outside banking hours. For the journey itself you will need enough for drinks and snacks – if driving through other countries you will need cash in the currencies of those countries for petrol and tolls. You should have means to pay any French on-the-spot fines (almost F1000 for speeding!) if you're driving through France. Cash will be needed, too, to buy a few basics on arrival.

Most banks hold only limited amounts of foreign currencies, so it is safest to give them two or three days' notice of your requirements. They only supply notes, not coins. Although it would be foolish to take all your holiday money as cash, it can be annoying (and expensive, if you are charged commission each time) to be constantly changing small amounts.

TRAVELLERS CHEQUES

Travellers cheques are the most popular way of taking money abroad. They are simple, safe and, provided you take a well known brand (American Express, Thomas Cook, or from one of the big banks) are accepted almost everywhere. The cheques can be in any currency – if you take them in lire you only need worry about the exchange rate when you buy, rather than when you use them (although if you are going through France beware of using lire travellers cheques, because you are then converting money yet again, and you will lose out). You can buy travellers cheques at banks, building societies and travel agents; you may be able to get them on the spot but it's advisable to order in advance, allowing about a week as they may have to be ordered from another branch. Banks charge around 1% commission on their travellers cheques but you may find that the building society rates are lower. Whoever collects the travellers cheques has to sign them in front of the cashier. On holiday they can then only be cashed or used by that signatory – not by partners, friends or grown-up children.

To cash travellers cheques on holiday you'll need your passport as a means of identification – cashiers are always on the look out for potential thieves. Shop around for the best place to exchange them as rates and commission charges vary as a general rule avoid late-night exchanges and hotels and stick to the larger banks where your sterling will go further.

The main advantage of travellers cheques is their refund service; facilities vary from issuer to issuer but lost or stolen cheques can usually be replaced or refunded within a reasonable period of time. Remember to keep a separate note of the cheque numbers and the issuer's emergency telephone number. If disaster strikes this will speed up the refund process. The disadvantage is that you pay for them when you collect them, so the money leaves your account immediately, as cash would.

For lost or stolen travellers cheques, see Chapter 12, EMERGENCIES.

EUROCHEQUES

If you have a cheque account, you can order a book of Eurocheques and a Eurocheque guarantee card. These cheques can be used throughout Europe to buy goods or to obtain cash (although there's usually a transaction charge for the latter). They are popular in Italy and are accepted almost everywhere. As with travellers cheques, shop around for the best rates and commissions when cashing them.

Unlike UK cheques, Eurocheques have space to write in the name of the appropriate currency – so you can write a cheque in French francs, Italian lire, German marks or whatever, as well as in sterling. The cheque is converted into sterling at the rate of exchange prevailing on the day that the cheque is processed by your bank, and deducted from your account along with a small handling charge. Places that accept them often display a sticker (a blue and red *ec* on a white background).

Once written and supported by a guarantee card a Eurocheque cannot be stopped – so it is extremely important to keep cheques and card apart or you could be in for heavy losses if they were stolen together.

If you know the personal identity number (PIN) for your Eurocheque card you may also be able to get money from cash dispensers, again look for the *ec*. The machines will guide you through the transaction in English, all you have to do is tap in your PIN and the amount of foreign currency you require.

Eurocheques are provided free on request by most banks although you'll be charged a small annual fee for the card.

Try to order them well in advance as it may take a few weeks for the card and your PIN to reach you.

CREDIT CARDS

Credit and charge cards are a useful way of paying for goods and services on holiday and, provided you can afford to pay off the balance within the specified period, they also make financial good sense. The two main limitations with credit cards are that you have to stick to your pre-set spending limit although you may be able to get this raised for the duration of your holiday; also they are frequently not accepted at petrol stations in Italy.

On the whole you are likely to get a better rate of exchange with a credit card or charge card than with other forms of holiday money because the credit card issuer can afford to deal at more competitive rates than the individual. You'll be able to obtain cash on your card at larger banks and from some cash dispenser machines where you see the credit card logo. Another plus is that many of the major credit card/charge card issuers operate a guarantee service for anything paid for by the card. However, don't rely solely on your credit or charge card, especially in out-of-the-way places. Credit card fraud is increasing in Italy, so don't be surprised if you're asked for some other form of identification (passport) when you pay. And always check that the card returned is yours – substitution of an out-of-date card is not unheard of. For lost or stolen credit cards see Chapter 12, EMERGENCIES.

TAKING YOUR CAR – THE PRACTICALITIES

DOCUMENTS

Driving licence If you are going to drive through France, you must be 18 or over and in possession of a full EC UK driving licence. Drivers who have held their licence for less than one year must keep to a maximum speed of 90km/h (about 52mph) and display a '90' sign on the rear of the vehicle. Signs are available from most petrol stations in France.

In Italy itself, it is recommended that you carry an international driving licence. This is available from the AA and RAC to holders of a full UK driving licence who are over 18. The international licence is recommended for holders of the pink EC UK licence. If you have a green UK licence, you can obtain free a translation into Italian of the wording on the licence from a motoring organization – carry it together with your licence. The Italians don't recognize the green UK licence without this translation.

Vehicle registration document You must carry the original registration document of your vehicle. If the vehicle is not registered in your name you should carry a letter from the owner giving you permission to drive. It is routine practice in many European countries for police to check the vehicle's papers as well as the driver's licence, if they stop a car for any reason, and carrying the registration document in the car is obligatory. (If you hire a car you will be given all the documentation.)

Nationality plate You must display a GB nationality sticker on the rear of your vehicle. The oval sticker should be 17.5cm (7in) by 11.5cm (4½in) with black letters on a white background. Most insurance companies, motoring organizations and ferry companies will provide a free GB sticker.

Special note on boats It is advisable to obtain a Certificate of Registration if you are taking your boat abroad. Further details of the Certificate can be obtained from the Royal Yachting Association (see USEFUL ADDRESSES at the end of Chapter 3).

INSURANCE

Everyone driving in Italy must be insured. Your UK policy will provide overseas cover to satisfy the statutory minimum requirements in Italy. However, this is unlikely to match even third party cover in the UK – so no personal, damage, fire or theft cover is included even if you have a fully comprehensive policy. It's best to give your insurers a ring to check their specific recommendations – it will probably be a Green Card.

Green Card This is strongly recommended for Italy, and it could prove useful in France, too. Most insurance companies will issue a Green Card free of charge for a set period. In the event of an accident, this card will assist in proving that you are insured. It will also assist in extending the cover your UK policy provides in Italy.

Transit insurance Most car insurance provides cover for transit from UK ports. You will need to check the extent of the policy if you wish to travel on ferries outside the UK.

THE CAR

Get it serviced, and check tyres.

Headlights Your headlights should be converted for driving abroad by using either headlamp convertors or beam deflectors.

Car telephones Many countries exercise control over the importation and use of car telephones. It will probably be useless anyway. For further details contact your phone network, a motoring organization or Tourist Office.

EXTRA EQUIPMENT

It is strongly recommended that you take the following equipment when driving in Italy. The items are available from large garages, accessory shops and motoring organizations:

- red warning triangle – this is compulsory for your drive through France unless the vehicle has hazard warning lights.

However, it is strongly recommended, as an accident may render the vehicle's electronics useless. It is also compulsory in Italy

- spare bulb kit (compulsory in Italy)
- headlamp converter/deflector
- first aid kit
- left and right external mirror (the left-hand wing mirror is essential when driving on the right)
- fire extinguisher

HOLIDAY HEALTH

If you're already taking prescribed medicines make sure you have enough to last the whole holiday and take a copy of the prescription with you just in case.

Your GP will be able to tell you whether you require any booster injections or vaccinations for the trip, will also be able to prescribe any special medical supplies you'll need and advise you on taking very young children abroad. If you or anyone in your family has a serious medical condition ask your doctor to give you a note of explanation to carry with you. A note is also important in the case of allergies, such as to penicillin.

It's a good idea to try to carry a prescription for spectacles, too, just in case yours meet with an accident.

As far as teeth go, toothache and a hunt for a dentist can ruin a holiday, so if you're due for a check it's a good idea to have it before you go.

Most holiday ills are a result of over-exposure to the sun and unaccustomed food (see HEALTH, Chapter 11). Buy and use plenty of high-factor suncream.

FIRST AID KIT

A good first aid kit is essential on holiday. When travelling, make sure you keep it to hand. A kit should include the following – you may prefer to buy a ready-made kit and add to it yourself.

- adhesive plasters
- assorted bandages
- absorbent lint
- cotton wool
- antiseptic creams
- disinfectant
- calamine lotion/sunburn creams
- insect bite cream/repellent
- travel sickness tablets
- pain relief tablets, such as aspirin
- scissors

- safety pins
- tweezers
- thermometer
- any medicines prescribed by your GP

HAYFEVER

Acute sufferers will probably want to head for coastal regions where on-shore winds will disperse the local pollen. Even if you think you've found a pollen-free retreat take medication with you as familiar brands may not be available.

If you'd like more information on how to plan a hayfever-free trip you can send for the *Holidays without Hayfever Report*. Write to: Dr Jean Emberlin, Pollen Research Unit, Geography Department, Polytechnic of North London, 383 Holloway Road, London N7 8DB.

USEFUL ADDRESSES

The Department of Health's leaflet, *The Traveller's Guide To Health* (form T1) which includes further information about the E111 and claiming sickness benefits abroad is available at post offices along with form E111. Alternatively you can write to: Health Publications Unit, No.2 Site, Heywood Stores, Manchester Road, Heywood, Lancashire OL10 2PZ, or phone free on 0800 555 777. People living in Northern Ireland should should write to the address below for information, advice or form E111: Department of Health and

Social Services, Overseas Branch, Lindsay House, 8–14 Callender Street, Belfast BT1 5DP.

The following may be able to offer general advice on holiday health including vaccinations; British Airways Travel Clinics: contact 071 831 5333 for details of your nearest clinic; MASTA – Medical Advisory Service for Travellers Abroad 071 631 4408; Trailfinders Medical Centre 071 938 3999; Thomas Cook Medical Centre 071 408 4157.

AT HOME

- arrange for pets to be cared for while you're away
- cancel milk/papers
- unplug all electrical appliances
- deposit special valuables in the bank
- ask someone to keep an eye on your house/water the plants, remove visible mail, etc.
- inform the DSS that you're going abroad if you're receiving any form of benefit, as it may be affected.

WHAT TO TAKE

The lists below provide an average sort of checklist – they will inevitably be too long for some readers, too short for others. It is practical to take some items below only if you are driving.

TRAVEL

- passports
- travel documents – e.g. tickets, insurance certificates
- money – travellers cheques, Eurocheques, credit cards, etc. (make a note of numbers and keep them separately). Check credit card spending limits are sufficient if you're planning to use them while away, otherwise you may prefer to leave them at home.

HEALTH AND TOILETRIES

- prescriptions – for medicines, contact lenses, glasses
- first-aid kit – see HOLIDAY HEALTH, above
- travel sickness tablets
- contraception
- tampons
- contact lens solutions
- small mirror
- toiletries
- insect repellent
- sun protection
- moist wipes

USEFUL SUNDRIES

- sheets and pillowcases, unless you are hiring them
- towels and beachtowels
- plastic bags
- small sewing kit
- alarm clock
- torch – at least one if you're staying in the country
- adjustable spanner (you may need it for gas bottles)
- screwdriver (there may be one in the house – but you'll know where yours is!)
- guide books/good phrase book
- back packs and/or money belts: useful for carrying maps and valuables once you're there
- holiday reading
- radio/cassette player and cassettes
- camera/films
- calculator (useful for converting currencies)
- scissors
- pen knife
- string
- continental plug adaptor for electrical appliances
- roll of lavatory paper
- pen and paper
- plug-in mosquito device (Boots and similar stores)

- waterproof clothing. Violent summer storms sometimes blow up on the coast or in the mountains. The Italian spring and autumn can be stormy too, and it has been known to rain for days in midsummer

FOR BABIES AND YOUNG CHILDREN

- disposable nappies: but don't take supplies for the whole holiday – you'll be able to buy them when you get there
- baby toiletries
- wipes
- bibs
- feeding cup/bottles (if your baby still needs a sterilized bottle you could take bottles with disposable, pre-sterilized liners/ teats)
- jars of favourite baby food
- hat (with an all-round brim to shield the neck) or sun-shade
- high factor sun-protection cream: see HEALTH in Chapter 11
- travel games
- toys
- wellington boots
- stick-on sun shade for the car (your own or a hire car)
- familiar bedding for very little ones

FOR THE KITCHEN

Your kitchen in Italy may be sparsely equipped, although any small essentials can always be bought. The following may prove useful, and you may use some items if you drive out. There are limits to what you can take if flying, of course.

- airtight containers
- vacuum flask
- cool bag (for picnics)
- plastic cups
- favourite sharp knife/potato peeler
- corkscrew/bottle opener
- tin-opener
- kitchen scissors

- measuring jug (calibrated in grams and ounces)
- safety matches
- foil/cling film
- a few plastic bags/dustbin bags

If you can't survive without them. . .

- egg cups
- tea pot/strainer
- pepper mill

FOOD

It's only worth taking food to cater for personal addictions of the tea, Marmite, marmalade variety. See Chapters 6 and 7 about food in Italy.

CHAPTER FIVE

WELCOME TO ITALY

The precise arrangements for arrival will be different from one house to another, and you should find out the procedure before you depart. Perhaps you will have to pick up keys from an office; maybe you will be met by an English agent or the caretaker; the owner might be on site; or – just as likely – you may be on your own with no-one to show you around.

INVENTORY

One of the things you will have to tackle is the inventory – you may be expecting to hand over a deposit at this stage, to be returned when you leave.

The vocabulary below should help with the inventory:

ampolle	cruet
apriscatole	tin-opener
asciugamano	bath towel
bacinella	basin
bicchiere	glass
bilancia	scales
bollitore	kettle
bombola del gas	gas cylinder
branda	folding bed
brocca	water jug
caffettiera	coffee machine
capezzale	bolster
caraffa	decanter

carta igienica	lavatory paper
cavatappi	corkscrew
cistola	cereal bowl
coltello da cucina	kitchen knife
contenitore del pane	bread bin
coperchio	lid
coperta	blanket
cucchiaio	spoon
cuccetta	bunk
cuscino	pillow
fornello	cooker
frullino	whisk
grattugia	cheese grater
imbuto	funnel
insalatiera	salad bowl
lampadina	light bulb
lenzuolo	sheet
letto matrimonale	double bed
letto singolo	single bed
macinacaffè	coffee grinder
macinapepe	pepper mill
mannaia	meat cleaver
materasso	mattress
matterello	rolling pin
mestolo	ladle
padella	frying pan
patumiera	dustbin
pentola	saucepan
pietanza	dish
piattino	saucer
piattino per il burro	butter dish
piatto	plate
piumino	eiderdown
portacenere	ashtray
portauovo	egg cup
saliera	salt cellar
scodella	mug

scolapasta	collander
scolapiatti	plate rack
scopa	broom
sottopiatto	table mat
tappetino	bathroom mat
tappeto	carpet
teiera	tea pot
tostapane	toaster
trinciante	carving knife
vasellane	crockery
vaso	vase
vassoio	tray

If someone *is* there to show you what's what, they will most probably have a routine for showing how awkward equipment works – still, the chances are they will just have left as you discover that you only have one set of keys for six people, or some other inconvenience.

Therefore (though we're not suggesting that you ask all the questions below!) it may be worth having a quick run-through on the basics before the owner, caretaker or agent disappears, or at any rate before nightfall. (The list appears phrasebook-style in case you need to ask in Italian.)

THINGS TO ASK THE CARETAKER/AGENT

May we check a few things before you go, please?
Possiamo controllare alcune cose prima che lei se ne vada?

Where's the best place to park the car?
Dov'è il parcheggio migliore per la macchina?

How does this work, please?
Come funziona?

doors/keys	*porte/chiavi*
windows	*finestre*

shutters	*persiane*
shower	*doccia*
oven	*forno*
washing machine	*lavatrice*
lights	*luci*
telephone	*telefono*
water cold/hot	*acqua fredda/calda*
air conditioning	*l'aria condizionata*
lavatory	*gabinetto*

Could you let us have some more . . . please?
Potrebbe darci altra/altre/altri . . . per favore?

keys	*chiavi*
pillows	*cuscini*
pillowcases	*federe*
sheets	*lenzuola*
blankets/duvets	*coperte/piumini*
towels (these may not be provided, of course)	*asciugamani*
lavatory paper	*carta igienica*
light bulbs	*lampadine*
coat hangers	*grucce*
cutlery	*posate*
crockery	*vasellame*
glasses	*bicchieri*

Where should we put the rubbish?
Dove buttiamo la spazzatura?

Which way to the. . . ?
Come si va al/alla/all' . . . ?

Is it open tomorrow?
Sarà aperto/aperta domani?

supermarket	*il supermercato*
shop	*il negozio*
baker	*il panificio*
bank/exchange	*la banca/cambio*

post office	*l'ufficio postale*
petrol station	*il rifornitore/il benzinaio*
tourist office	*l'ufficio informazioni turistiche*
pharmacy	*la farmacia*

Would you be able to arrange a babysitter for us?
Ci potrebbe trovare una babysitter?

Could you give us the name and address of a local doctor, please?
Potrebbe darci il nome e l'indirizzo di un medico in zona, per cortesia?

When does the cleaner come?
Quando viene la domestica?

Monday	*lunedì*
Tuesday	*martedì*
Wednesday	*mercoledì*
Thursday	*giovedì*
Friday	*venerdì*
Saturday	*sabato*
Sunday	*domenica*
daily	*ogni giorno*
morning/afternoon	*la mattina/il pomeriggio*

Where can we get in touch with you?
Dove possiamo metterci in contatto con lei?

BASIC SHOPPING STRAIGHT AWAY

Although some houses come complete with a 'welcome pack' of basics to get you started, you will probably arrive to discover that the cupboards are bare, and might like to stock up on a few basics straight away. (You may have brought some of these with you, of course, especially if you have travelled by car.) Most of the ideas on the list below will be found in the local supermarket or a general food shop although fruit and salad will probably be better from the

67

market, if you find one (see Chapter 7, SHOPPING FOR FOOD).

You may decide to eat out on your first evening, so the next day's breakfast will be your main concern. If you decide to cook at home, you could refer to the MENUS AND RECIPES section, where shopping lists are included.

mineral water (sparkling/still)	*acqua minerale (gassata/naturale)*
wine	*vino*
soft drinks	*bibite, analcolici*
orange juice	*succo d'arancia*
milk	*latte*
tea	*tè*
coffee	*caffè*
beer	*birra*
butter	*burro*
margarine	*margarina*
jam	*marmellata*
bread (this may be available fresh in the morning, although perhaps not on Sunday)	*pane*
breakfast cereal	*fiocchi d'avena*
cheese	*formaggio*
eggs	*uova*
cold meat	*affettati*
salad	*insalata*
vegetables	*verdure*
fruit	*frutta*
salt	*sale*
matches	*fiarmmiferi*
ant powder	*insetticida in polvere per le formiche*
lavatory paper	*carta igienica*
local map	*pianta della zona*

See also SURVIVAL SHOPPING (Chapter 11) if you discover you have forgotten something vital.

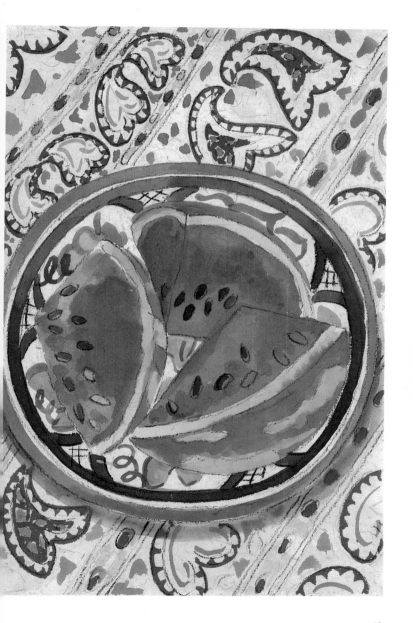

CHAPTER SIX

EATING AND DRINKING

The Italians are tremendously proud of their cooking. They aren't gluttons but they do understand the value of carefully prepared food and they revel in the unique enjoyment of a good meal shared with friends or family. Food is one of the great joys of the Italian way of life. If you decide to cook *alla maniera italiana* you'll find that many dishes are quick and easy to prepare – there's no need for long and laborious sessions in the kitchen.

If you decide to do your own shopping and cooking on holiday you'll find yourself learning a good deal about the traditions and the lifestyle that's going on around you. Eating and drinking in Italy is a kind of pleasant history lesson. It's little more than a hundred years since the country was united under a single government. Until then the peninsula was divided up into a number of independent states, each with its own culinary traditions. Although Garibaldi and the Risorgimento of 1861 brought political unity, cooks all over the country are still loyal to their own regional recipes. Naturally, some dishes became popular all over the country – although a dish from one area adopted by another was often given a local, dialect name.

The history of the different regions can be traced in some of their traditional dishes. In Sicily, for example, they eat a version of North African couscous – known as *cuscùs* – a legacy from the Arab occupation in the 9th and 10th centuries. Venetian cooking also tells a tale. For centuries Venice and her fleet held the monopoly of Oriental trade, bringing back the spices that were to become such an important ingredient in Italian cookery. When shiploads of maize began to arrive from newly discovered America it was Venetian cooks, accustomed to strange and exotic ingredients, who first converted it into *polenta*. *Polenta*, cooked in a myriad of different ways, is still a staple of Venetian cooking.

Naturally, regions with foreign borders tend to have absorbed some of their neighbours' culinary traditions. In the Trentino-Alto Adige Austrian influence is very strong. Many of the local dishes have German names and are served with sauerkraut or dumplings. Similarly, Piedmont has its own version of the Swiss fondue, called *fonduta*.

Wine and food are inseparable in Italy. Unlike the English, Italians don't really believe in drinking alcohol without food to go with it. You may see a workman throwing back a glass of red wine in a bar on a cold winter's morning but there's no equivalent to the English pub and the kind of drinking that goes with it.

Wine is the traditional drink with meals but there are all sorts of delicious soft drinks (see NON-ALCOHOLIC DRINKS).

THE ITALIAN DAY

Breakfast (*prima colazione*) is usually a simple affair. At home it may consist of a sweet *espresso* coffee or a *caffellatte* (milky coffee), accompanied by specially manufactured breakfast biscuits. Look out for biscuits made by Il Mulino, they come in a variety of different shapes and sizes, some of them specially 'designed' for breakfast consumption. Lots of people have an *espresso* in a bar on the way to work, which generally starts at eight. Italian-style *brioche* are the other staple breakfast food. You can buy these at a baker's if you want to have them for breakfast at home. They will either be filled with confectioner's custard (*crema*), or jam (*marmellata*). *Caffellatte* is also available at bars. It is less frothy than the *cappuccino*, and has more milk in proportion to coffee. Only foreigners choose to have these distinctly 'morning' drinks as the finale to a meal! There's another break a couple of hours later for a *cappuccino* and a sweet pastry. Between ten and eleven in the morning it's quite common to see large groups of men downing *cappuccini* and doughnuts with a custard filling (*bomba*).

Lunch (*il pranzo*), happens at about one o'clock. In small towns and villages people almost always eat at home. Offices – and shops as well in the smaller towns – close between one and three or even four o'clock. This allows ample time for a good meal and a *siesta*. Traditionally, northern Italians eat a large lunch and a light supper, while people in the South eat less during the heat of the day, reserving their main meal for the evening.

The evening meal is called *la cena*, and is eaten at about half past eight. The full Italian meal follows the same structure in most parts of the country, starting with the *antipasto* – a selection of cold meats and salami, vegetables and salads. This is followed by the *primo* – usually soup, pasta or a *risotto*. The main course (*il secondo*) will be meat or fish. The Italians don't use as many sauces and gravies as the English and French. Fish is often grilled over an open wood fire and served with nothing but a squeeze of lemon – delicious! Good cuts of meat are treated in a similar way. This method, which we would probably call 'barbecuing', is known as cooking *alla brace*. The main course is generally served on its own and followed by vegetables or salad. Fruit and cheese often follow this, as *dolci* (desserts) tend to be reserved for Sundays.

There's a popular image of Italians sitting down to enormous meals that last for hours and hours. Although Italy is the only country in which I've experienced a fourteen-course wedding banquet – we danced between courses – on the whole they're rather like the British, and only have large and elaborate meals on special occasions. Nowadays pasta and a salad followed by fruit and cheese is considered perfectly adequate. Meat and fish are no longer essential elements of every meal. The *fettina* (fried or grilled escalope), once a part of the staple diet, has been virtually abandoned by the younger generation. In MENUS AND RECIPES, Chapter 8, you'll find a mixture of light meals and more traditional ones with three courses.

Despite the modern tendency to eat slightly less, Sunday lunch continues to be a lengthy, family affair. Go to any small city on a Sunday morning and the streets and *piazzas* will be full of people carrying ornate confectioners' boxes. Carefully secured ribbons allow these boxes to be swung nonchalantly from one finger – they look more like the latest fashion accessory than the Sunday pudding wending its way home.

CAN WE DRINK THE WATER?

Although its generally safe to drink water straight from the tap all over the country, it's not always a pleasant experience. At best the water will be heavily chlorinated, and at worst it will have a distinctive smell all of its own! Anyone who's been to Florence will know exactly what I mean. Drought conditions in recent years have taken their toll on the supply of drinking water. Chlorination has increased and in some places the water is a pale, peaty brown. Still safe, but far from appetizing.

Occasionally you will see the words *acqua non potabile* over a tap or a fountain. This means that it's not drinking water. Taps on trains, for example, are always marked in this way. In the absence of a notice you can assume that the inviting drinking fountains that are to be seen on so many street corners, *piazzas* and station platforms are perfectly safe.

The Italians have been drinking bottled mineral water for much longer than we have. There's nothing fashionable about it, it's just a practical response to the problem of poor water. There are numerous different brands and each one lays claim to its own, health-giving properties. Some waters are so rich in minerals that they are quite unpalatable to the uninitiated – Ferrarelle is one to look out for on this score. Generally, however, mineral water simply tastes like water. It can be carbonated, either naturally or artificially (*acqua minerale gassata* or *acqua minerale frizzante*). If you prefer an uncarbonated water ask for *acqua minerale naturale*.

Uncarbonated mineral water can be useful for making up babies' bottles or reconstituting dried baby food. If you use tap water you should probably take the precaution of boiling or sterilizing it.

In a restaurant you'll automatically be served with mineral water. This can be a bit irritating if you're trying to save money. If you want a jug of tap water you should ask for *acqua dal rubinetto*. It may not taste good, but at least it's free!

On some of the off-shore islands water can be in short supply. In the South it has to be shipped out regularly in tankers from the mainland. It has been known to run out at the height of the holiday season, so buy plenty of mineral water while stocks last! On some of the southern islands your shower may be fed from a rainwater tank on the roof. The sun heats the water during the day and by the evening it's quite hot. This system usually works well, although I once found tiny, bleached bones raining down on my head with the shower water. They turned out to be all that remained of a bird that had slipped under the netting on the tank during the winter – we wished we hadn't been washing up with it all that time!

You may find that the kitchen sink in your house has three taps – two cold and one hot. One of the taps will be connected directly to the mains and this is the one that you should drink from. The other, which is fine for washing up, will draw water from the cold water tank in the roof. You may need to ask the caretaker which is which.

WINES, BEERS AND OTHER INTERESTING BOTTLES

NON-ALCOHOLIC DRINKS *(analcolici)*

If you don't want an alcoholic drink there are plenty of alternatives to choose from. Making *espresso* is the *raison d'être* of every bar. Each strong, black cup of it is made separately with a tremendous hissing and steaming. If you find *espresso* too strong you can ask to have a little extra water in it – *un espresso alto*, although it won't make a lot of difference if you're longing to quench your thirst. You may prefer to dilute it with brandy (*un caffè corretto*). *Cappuccino*, as everyone knows, is a frothy, milky coffee. If you prefer you can have *caffellatte*, which has more milk and less froth, or *caffè freddo* – strong black coffee served very cold in a glass. Tea is available at most bars. A tea bag on a long string will be lowered into a cup of boiling water. Don't expect high quality – you'll probably lose your taste for tea after a week or two. If they drink it at all, the Italians usually take lemon with their tea.

Bars usually sell a wide range of rather sweet bottled fruit juices. Varieties include peach, apricot and pear. You may prefer a freshly squeezed orange, lemon or grapefruit (*una spremuta di arancia/limone/pompelmo*). This will be served in a tall glass with a drop of mineral water, a sachet of sugar and a long teaspoon. *Spremuta* made from Sicilian blood oranges (*tarocchi*) is particularly impressive as it comes out bright red. Some bars make fresh fruit milkshakes – these are a speciality in Rome. In the evenings or during cooler weather you might enjoy a rich hot chocolate (*cioccolata*). At its best this tastes like pure chocolate that's been melted down and mixed with cream – delicious!

It's quite acceptable to order an *analcolico* (non-alcoholic aperitif) in a bar or restaurant. Aperol is a well known non-alcoholic bitter.

USEFUL WORDS AND PHRASES

a bottle	*una bottiglia*
hot chocolate	*cioccolata calda*
freshly squeezed fruit juice	*spremuta*
fruit juice	*succo di frutta*
a glass	*un bicchiere*
milkshake	*un frulatte*
non-alcoholic	*analcolico*
tea with milk	*un tè con latte*
tea with lemon	*tè al limone*
with water	*con acqua*

WINE *(vino)*

If you're planning to 'live as the Romans' this holiday could be an opportunity for some serious wine tasting. Wine buffs should set their reservations aside and discover the delights and intricacies of Italian wine in its own setting.

Italy produces more wine every year than anywhere else in the world. This makes for a variety that can be rather bewildering. It may help you to know that some wines are named after the place of production – a vineyard, a village, town or region. Others bear the name of the grape they are made of – Sangiovese, Aleatico, Moscato, Nebbiolo or Pinot being some examples. Just to confuse matters there are several wines with fantastic names that seem to bear no relation to anything. At the end of this section on wines, you'll find a brief glossary of wine words that may help you to identify what you want.

As a general rule it's worth approaching the question of wine in much the same way as food. Find out what's being produced locally and stick to that as your *vino da tavola* or table wine for everyday consumption. If it's what local people drink it's bound to be good. Wine and food are inseparable in Italy. It's hard to say whether recipes were originally developed to complement the wine or vice versa. Whatever the sequence you'll find that the local vintage marries perfectly with any regional recipes that you care to try – a useful guide when you want to find a wine to go with a recipe from Chapter 8.

If you're staying in a wine growing area you can usually buy direct from a producer. Ask the caretaker of your house where to go: *C'è una fattoria dove posso comprare del vino?* She may even be able to sell you some herself. If there isn't a caretaker you could try asking at the local shop or bar. Failing that, look out for signs on the road saying *vendita diretta del vino*. Take some bottles or plastic containers with you. You'll probably be invited to taste a selection before making your choice. This could be a memorable experience or, in extreme cases, an experience that you can't remember at all.

You should ask whether a wine will travel well before buying some to take back to England: *Questo vino si sciuperà in viaggio?* A general rule is that simple, local wines don't stand up well to extremes of temperature and prolonged movement, so don't take these back with you. Something that was cheap and delicious in its own setting can prove unpalatable at home. In compensation, the purity of these rustic wines will allow you to drink enormous quantities while you are in the area, without even a trace of a hangover to cloud your holiday.

If you are staying in one of the great wine producing areas – Tuscany, Piedmont or the Veneto – you'll find signs for the 'wine route' or *strada del vino*. This will lead you past the principal vineyards and outlets (*enoteche*). Buying wine from an *enoteca* is quite a formal affair, but you'll be able to taste it just the same.

In other regions you can buy local, unpretentious wines from the grocer (*alimentari*). Ask for *il vino della zona*. Larger towns and cities will have a wine merchant which will be called the *enoteca* or *negozio di vini e liquori*.

It's worth looking out for the letters DOC (*Denominazione di Origine Controllata*) on a bottle. Although not a guarantee of quality, it means that the producer has conformed to various governmental rules about the method of production and the alcohol content of his wine. However, if you're looking for really fine wines DOCG (*Denominazione di Origine Controllata e Garantita*) is the mark to look out for. These bottles do carry a guarantee of quality. They have been sampled and passed by a panel of official wine tasters. So far this 'top category' label has been awarded to only five wines: Barbaresco, Barolo, Brunello di Montalcino, Chianti and Vino Nobile di Montepulciano.

While we're on the subject of quality, don't be lured into buying cheap bottles of blended wines from the supermarket – you're bound to regret it the following morning. They can often be identified by their metal tops – although Lambrusco is an exception to the rule.

REGIONAL WINES

The north-west

Much of Italy is too hot to produce really fine wines. However, Piedmont in the north-west of the country lies at the foot of the Alps and, incidentally, on the same latitude as the Rhône valley. The heat of the summer sun is not so extreme here as in other Italian vine growing regions further south. This slightly more temperate climate combined with ideal soils and generations of experience produces some of Italy's finest wines.

The famous red wines of Piedmont, such as Barolo and Barbaresco, tend to be very full-bodied. They are often compared with the French Rhône wines. Barolo, which was among the first wines to earn the DOCG title, is thought by some people to be one of the finest red wines in the world. It's made from the Nebbiolo grape and comes from the hills that surround the comune of Barolo near Alba. (Alba, the home of chocolates, white truffles and fine red wines is a hedonist's paradise.) A minimum of three years in a cask before bottling produces a very full flavoured, fruity red wine with a fine, deep colour and a minimum alcohol content of 13%. Traditionally it's said to have a bouquet of violets and tar. You'd be wise to stand the bottle upright the day before you plan to drink it – this will allow the sediment to settle. Allow it to breathe for a couple of hours before the meal and then pour it carefully so that you won't disturb the sediment. Ideally Barolo should be served with hearty red meat dishes or game.

Barbaresco, another DOCG fine wine, is made from the Nebbiolo grape in Barbaresco to the east of Alba. Like Barolo it's a full-bodied, fragrant red. However, it matures slightly more quickly than Barolo, and is drier and not quite so strong. As it ages Barbaresco aquires a beautiful amber tinge.

Although it hasn't earnt DOCG status, Barbera completes the big red Piedmontese trio. Named after one of the most prolific grapes of the region it doesn't have to be taken quite so seriously as the other two. It's a lighter wine with a tendency to be slightly sweet. It can be anything from *frizzante* to fully sparkling. Knock it back without too much reverence while you're eating pasta dishes or meat cooked in a tomato sauce.

Dolcetto is another good, everyday red wine. Like Barbera it can have a refreshing tingle and it marries well with anything from *antipasti* to fruit and cheese. Grattinara completes the list of fine Piedmontese reds. Like Barolo it's made from the Nebbiolo grape. Some people prefer it to Barolo – they say that it has a greater depth and richness than the more famous wine.

Not content with creating some of Italy's finest red wines Piedmont also produces Asti Spumante – probably the most popular sparkling white wine in the world. It's a delicate, slightly sweet wine made from Moscato grapes. Some people find Asti a bit too sweet, but served with fruit or a dessert it's ideal and is enlivening at the end of a meal. Moscato d'Asti is similar to the spumante, although the alcohol content is lower and so is the price.

Finally, to crown its attributes as the ideal holiday destination for wine lovers from all over the world, Piedmont produces most of Italy's Vermouth. Turin is the centre of the industry and it is here that Cinzano, Martini and Carpano are based.

Lombardy's best known wines are red. The Valtelline in the north of the region, just below the Swiss border, is the most important area for wine production. There is something surprising about seeing thriving vines at a height of two and a half thousand feet above sea level. However, it's from the Nebbiolo grape grown on these high terraces that Sassella, Grumello and Inferno are made. Sassella, a light, refreshing red, is generally thought to be the best of the three. All the Valtelline wines are a brilliant ruby red when poured and they go well with any kind of roast or grilled meat.

The north-east

Technically the beautiful Alpine region of Alto Adige is part of Trentino. However, its inhabitants are largely German speaking and the wines have German names. They used to be made almost entirely for export to Austria and Switzerland, remaining virtually unknown in the rest of Italy. However, things started to change in the early 1980s when the traditional foreign markets declined and, because of Common Market membership, the wines of Alto Adige began to be sold within Italy.

The Schiava grape, used to make the reds in this region, produces light wines such as Santa Maddalena and Lago di Caldaro. Santa Maddalena, said to be the superior of the two, is a light and very drinkable wine that is sometimes almost rosé in colour. Although the whites in this area are often made from the grapes of German varieties of vine, they are said never to taste quite the same on this side of the border. Look out for the Reisling which is light, delicate and sometimes quite dry – a perfect drink at the height of summer. The same goes for the fragrant products of the Müller-Thurgau and the rather sharper Sylvaner-based wines.

Trentino produces rather more wine than the Alto Adige. Teroldego, made from a grape of the same name, is a robust red with an almost nutty flavour. Marzemino, also named after the grape, received early publicity from Mozart's librettist who referred to it in *Don Giovanni* as '*l'eccelente Marzemino*'. It's another full-bodied red that would go well with a *bistecca* (steak) or an *arrosto* (roast). Among the whites Moscato (Muscat), Pinot Grigio, Chardonnay and Sauvignon are the ones to try. For a special occasion, round the meal off with one of the luscious sweet Moscatos. Moscato Rosa, or Rosenmuskateller, is described by experts as one of the world's greatest sweet wines.

In Friuli-Venezia Giulia, Picolit takes the place of Moscato as a dessert wine. It is golden in colour and is said to have been a popular drink in the court of Queen Victoria. Tocai, a light, dry white, is the perfect partner for fish. Finally, you should sample some of the delicious local Verduzzo. You'll soon discover that this white wine can be sweet, dry, or even *frizzante*, according to the whim of the producer.

Along with Tuscany and Piedmont, the Veneto is one of the main wine producing and exporting regions in the country. This is the home of the 'big three' – Soave, Valpolicella and Bardolino. Italy exports more bottles of Soave each year than any other wine. Named after a town in the hills between Verona and Vicenza, it's made largely from Garganega grapes. Good Soave – the kind you'll find in its native setting – is a sharp, dry white with a flowery bouquet. Serve it very cool and you'll find that it goes beautifully with fish. Prosecco, another white, is a dry, sparkling wine from the area around Conegliano. Recently it has ousted the more traditional Martinis and Camparis as a fashionable aperitif.

The reds, Bardolino and Valpolicella, have virtually achieved the status of household names in Britain. They are both made from a mixture of Corvina and Negrara grapes. The vines used for Bardolino grow on the shores of Lake Garda, while Valpolicella is produced in the hills. Valpolicella is the slightly fuller flavoured of the two but, like Bardolino, it responds well to being chilled. A young Bardolino is often slightly *frizzante* – which makes it a pleasant drink with a light, summer supper.

Central Italy

Chianti Classico is one of Italy's most famous red wines. The beautiful Tuscan hill country known as the Chianti covers an area of about two hundred square miles. It corresponds to an autonomous region of the 14th century known as the League of Chianti. Today, only the wine of the area that meets a certain standard can bear the identifying mark of the *gallo nero* – a black cockerel on a gold background. As a young wine it's fresh and fruity and can even have a slight prickle to it. As it matures it takes on a fuller, deeper flavour. Predictably, Chianti Classico is delicious when drunk with the simple dishes of the region.

Each autumn the *consorzi*, or wine producers' cooperatives, in the Chianti arrange a walk of 30km (20 miles) or so known as the Marcia nel Chianti. If you happen to be near Siena in September, try to go. The route, although different each year, is invariably beautiful. You'll be awarded a bottle of Chianti for completing the course – no mean feat with temperatures in the eighties.

A good deal of Chianti is made outside the 'Classico' region. Often the same mixture of grapes and an identical method of production produces a wine, Chianti Putto, that is so similar only the expert palate can distinguish from the Classico version. (*Putto* means 'cherub', but the wine itself is no baby!)

There are other important Tuscan wines as well as Chianti. Brunello di Montalcino and Vino Nobile de Montepulciano have both received the DOCG award. Brunello is produced in the area surrounding the hill town of Montalcino to the south of Siena. It's a big red wine, full of flavour and depth. It has to be aged for at least four years before being released for sale and even then it's not really ready to drink. If you want a bottle of Brunello for a special occasion make sure that it's at least ten years old. Allow the sediment to settle for a day or two and then let it breathe for at least two hours before the meal. If you've got a bottle left over, keep it – it will continue to improve for the next fifty years! Montepulciano is quite close to Montalcino and the Vino Nobile is another fine red wine. Like Brunello it's at its best when its had time to age and mellow in the bottle.

Among the white wines of Tuscany Vernaccia di San Gimignano is one of the best known. It is a crisp, dry wine that goes down well on a hot day.

Tuscany is also famous for its Vin Santo. This is a sweet, amber coloured dessert wine made from partially dried grapes. It's often served with *cantucci*, hard almond biscuits that can be dipped into the wine (see MENUS AND RECIPES, Chapter 8).

There isn't a great deal of wine produced in Umbria but

Orvieto, a white wine named after its place of production, is famous all over the world. Traditionally it was always an *abbocato* or medium sweet wine. Despite its sweetness Orvieto *abbocato* is light enough when chilled to go well with chicken or fish. The ever increasing popularity of dry whites has prompted the production of an Orvieto *secco* as well. With its flowery bouquet and curious, bitter aftertaste this is said to be one of the most enjoyable Italian whites.

Emilia Romagna has made frothing wines into a speciality, and Lambrusco is the world's best selling wine. A dry, evanescent red, it stands as an exception to the rule about avoiding bottles without corks. You'll find that the lightness of Lambrusco combines perfectly with the rather rich cuisine of the area. If you want something with a bit more body try Sangiovese di Romagna. Albana Dolce is a sweet white dessert wine that is produced all over the region.

Verdicchio, which ranks with Soave, Orvieto and Frascati as one of Italy's best known dry white wines, comes from Le Marche. Just as the name implies, the wine has green (*verde*) reflections in some lights. Verdicchio dei Castelli di Jesi is the best known version. Le Marche is also famous for its Vin Santo (see Tuscany above).

In Lazio there are two main wine growing areas. The first, in the Alban hills south-east of Rome, is known as the Castelli Romani. Frascati is the best known wine from this area. It's a light, fresh tasting wine with a curious liquoricey aftertaste. The other important wine growing area is to the north of Rome around Lake Bolsena. This is the home of Est! Est! Est! – another white. The name of this wine comes from the legend that, when he travelled, a certain 12th-century bishop always sent his majordomo on ahead to test the wines. The man's job was to write '*Est*' on the door of any hostelry where the wine was good. When he tasted the wine of Montefiascone he was moved to scrawl '*Est! Est! Est!*' across the door of the tavern – a message that was sure to stop the bishop in his tracks . . .

In Abruzzi the vines are often used to produce grapes for

the table. Montepulciano d'Abruzzo, which can be red or rosé, is the best known wine of the region. Take care with the red – it can have an alcohol content of anything up to 18%!

The South and the islands

Wine production in the South is prolific. There are plenty of good, hearty table wines, although nothing to compare with the fine wines of northern Italy.

Puglia in the south-east produces more wine than any other region in Italy. Traditionally most of the red is used for blending and the whites serve as a base for vermouth. However, times are changing and Puglia is beginning to concentrate on quality as well as quantity. The Salentino peninsula to the south of Brindisi produces a rich, subtle red of the same name. Of the white wines San Savero, a fine, delicate white, is probably the best.

Campania's best known wine is Lacrima Cristi (Tears of Christ). It's a delicate, dry white with a hint of sweetness. You'll find that it goes well with fish. According to local legend a German expert tasting it for the first time fell to his knees with the words 'Oh Christ! Why didn't You cry in Germany?' You may be disappointed to learn that the romantic name actually refers to the *lacrima* or teardrop method of vinification. Tarausi, which is made in the hills near Avellino, is a big red which some would go as far as comparing to Barolo. If you want a real treat try Tarausi Riserva.

Basilicata and Calabria aren't great wine producers. However, Calabrian Ciro is a good, robust, fruity red which often finds its way abroad.

In Sicily and Sardinia you will find an enormous variety of wines to choose from. Sicilian Corvo, which can be red or white, stands out from the crowd. It's a clear, light dry wine which is reputed to have medicinal qualities. The wines of Sardinia, like everything else on this beautiful island, are quite individual. Dry whites are served as dessert wines, sweet ones are drunk as aperitifs and the reds are known as

vini neri or black wines. Vermentino, a delicious dry white, is the best Sardinian wine. It has such a bitter finish that it can double up as an aperitif – rather like a dry sherry – and an accompaniment to the *antipasti* or fish as a main course.

An extraordinary range of sweet dessert wines also come from this area. The best known is probably the Sicilian Marsala that plays such an important role in recipes from all over the country. Like so many of these fortified wines, it's made from grapes that have been partially dried on the vine before picking. Dark and caramelly in flavour, it's somewhat reminiscent of Madeira. If you want to drink Marsala as well as splashing it into your cooking you should only buy the *vergine* or *superiore* qualities. The other versions, which will have been artificially sweetened with non-vinous substances, are best avoided.

The beautiful volcanic Eolian islands off Sicily are famous for their version of Malvasia, the golden dessert wine that can be found all over Italy. Malvasia di Lipari is the best. It manages to be sweet without cloying and has a bouquet of fresh fruit. To complete the list of white dessert wines, try the rich, sweet Moscato that is made all over the South and Sicily. In Puglia they produce highly alcoholic red dessert wines from the Primitivo grape. These will be of particular interest to anyone with a knowledge of Californian wines as the Primitivo is said to be an ancestor of California's Zinfandel.

USEFUL WORDS AND PHRASES

abboccato	smooth and slightly sweet wine
amabile	medium sweet
annata	year of production
bianco	white
classico	the best wine from a specified zone of production
DOC	wine from a specified area that meets certain standards

DOCG	as above, but passed by a panel of tasters
dolce	sweet
frizzante	slightly sparkling
grado alcolico	alcohol content
imbottigliato all'origine	bottled by the producer
invecchiato	aged
normale	non-*riserva*
passito	srong, sweet wine made from grapes that are dried or partially dried on the vine
profumato	aromatic
riserva	wine aged for at least three years
rosso	red
secco	dry
selezionato	selected for high quality
spumante	sparkling wine made from muscat grapes
stravecchio	very old
superiore	wine aged for a minimum statutory period
vecchio	old
vino da pasto/vino da tavola	ordinary table wine
vino vecchio	wine that has been aged

APERITIFS, LIQUEURS AND SPIRITS *(aperitivi e digestivi)*

Go to the bar for a leisurely aperitif before your meal. If you sit at a pavement table you'll be able to watch the evening *passegiata* when everyone seems to turn out for a stroll along the main street and a chat. In young and fashionable circles a glass of chilled Prosecco – sparkling white wine – often takes the place of a more traditional aperitif. Nevertheless, Campari, served with a dash of soda and a slice of lemon, is still very popular. If you haven't tasted it before, brace yourself for something really bitter. It's made from the peel of bitter oranges and quinine bark. Vermouth is easier on the palate. Martini, Cinzano and Carpano are the main brands. Of the red Martinis Punt e Mes is the most popular and has a distinctive, rather bitter taste. Legend has it that the drink was popular in a cafe near to the Stock Exchange in Turin. On one occasion the waiter found himself confronted with an excited broker shouting *'punt e mes, punt e mes'* (point and a half, point and a half) – obviously the crux of the business deal that he was struggling to arrange! From that day foward the drink was always known by this name.

Cynar is served with soda and a slice of lemon as an aperitif. It's made, rather surprisingly, from the essence of artichokes and has an odd, bitter-sweet flavour.

A good meal is always followed by a *digestivo* – a digestive or herbal liqueur. Again, you'll find that Italians often leave the house or restaurant where they've been eating to drink their *digestivo* at a bar. Amaro is probably the most popular. It comes in numerous varieties, all of them intensely and uncompromisingly bitter. Amaro Averna, produced in the South, Ramazzotti and Fernet Branca are the best known brands. Most *amari* are also advertised as pick-me-ups for the morning after – presumably having failed to do their job the night before.

Sambuca is another herbal liqueur. It tastes of aniseed and traditionally it's served *con mosche* or 'with flies'. The 'flies' are three coffee beans which are roasted *in situ* when a match is applied to the surface of the liqueur.

Grappa is a kind of firewater distilled from the skins, pips and stalks of grapes that have already been pressed to make wine. Every region has its own version and they are all tremendously strong – be particularly wary with the home made sort!

Cynar (see above) can also be drunk neat as a *digestivo* as can all the herbal liqueurs such as Strega and Fior d'Alpi. These are both made from a mixture of herbs and flowers soaked in spirit. Strega is sometimes compared to Benedictine.

Italy makes its own brandy – nearly all of it is produced by big, commercial concerns like Stock and Buton. Whisky is popular too. A good deal of it is imported but there are several Italian Scotch lookalikes.

BEER *(birra)*

The national beer is called Birra Peroni Nastro Azzuro. It was one of the first 'designer' beers to be imported into England. The usual bottled and canned lagers from Denmark and Germany are available everywhere. Some bars also have draught beers.

EATING OUT

RISTORANTI AND TRATTORIE

There are two main classes of restaurant in Italy, the *ristorante* and the *trattoria*, but there isn't always a great deal of difference between them. In theory the *ristorante* is the more formal of the two: the menu and wine list can be more elaborate, the tablecloths are starched and the waiters may wear white jackets. You'll pay slightly more for these trimmings.

There's usually a menu displayed on the wall outside both restaurants and *trattorie*. Although it's unlikely to include everything that's on offer, it will give you an idea of the prices. Have a look at it before going inside – there's nothing worse than having to change your mind after you've sat down. It's usually best to avoid restaurants that are empty – if local people don't like a place it probably means that it's overpriced or the food is poor. Mind you, you can't judge popularity before either one o'clock in the afternoon or eight at night – these are the times that the real trade begins. In small towns or villages the *trattoria* may only be open at lunchtime so don't be caught out.

Many *trattorie* advertise *la cucina casalinga*. This means much the same as 'good home cooking' and that's exactly what you can expect to get. There isn't always a printed menu. The faded scrap of paper on the wall outside will have given you some idea of the price and reassured you that there will be something to eat. However, once you're inside you probably won't see it again. The waiter, or possibly the cook himself, will simply reel off the dishes of the day. Don't be intimidated – it's not a listening comprehension test. If you don't understand ask him to repeat it: *può ripeterlo più lentamente, per favore?*. If all else fails, you can always ask for something appetizing that you can see another customer eating: *Mi piacerebbe mangiare quella pietanza per favore.*

If you eat at the *trattoria* there may well be a constant bustle of regular customers coming and going. Eating out is cheaper in Italy than England and a meal at a *trattoria* can be a matter of course rather than a special occasion. Regular customers will settle down with the newspaper while they wait for their meal or have a long chat with the *padrone* or restaurant owner. Don't expect rapid, American-style service. Eating in Italy is a form of relaxation. In all but the poorer, tourist restaurants the food is freshly prepared for each customer. You may have to wait for anything up to 20 minutes between courses but it will be worth it. Order some wine as soon as you arrive – it'll help you to get into the spirit of things.

THE OSTERIA

Strictly speaking, the *osteria* (called *hostaria* in Rome and the Lazio) or *locanda* is a country inn. However, there are plenty of *osterie* in the city. They're usually places where you can enjoy a drink and have a snack or light meal as well – a good place for sitting quietly in a corner and watching the real Italian world go by.

THE TAVOLA CALDA

The self service restaurant or *tavola calda* is a good place to go for a quick, straightforward lunch or light supper. The food is usually well prepared and reasonably priced. It's less of a linguistic challenge than the restaurant as you'll usually be able to help yourself to whatever you want.

BARS

You'll find that most bars can produce a snack lunch – a roll filled with salami, ham or cheese or rather delicate sandwiches made with sliced white bread and called *tramezzini* – not very filling but good with an aperitif. Toasted sandwiches (*tosti*) made with cheese or cheese and ham are often on offer, and so are slices of pizza. Pastries are also sold in bars. In a large bar you'll be expected to pay for what you want at the till (*la cassa*) before you eat it. Armed with your receipt (*lo scontrino*) you can then help yourself from the display counter. In small bars things may be less formal – you can usually eat first and pay afterwards.

Even the smallest of bars can offer the full range of alcoholic drinks at any time of day. Two or three shelves on the back wall are laden with an array of liqueurs, aperitifs, spirits and wines. (See NON-ALCOHOLIC DRINKS and APERITIFS, LIQUEURS AND SPIRITS in the previous section.)

If the tables outside the bar overlook a beautiful *piazza* or a lively street it's often worth paying extra to sit down for your drinks. Sometimes the bill is almost doubled on account of this privilege, so beware!

USEFUL WORDS AND PHRASES

an aperitif	*un'aperitivo*
a beer	*una birra*
a bottle	*una bottiglia*
draught beer	*una birra alla spina*
double	*doppio*
a glass	*un bicchiere*
a liqueur	*un liquore digestivo*
neat	*liscio*
on the rocks	*con ghiaccio*
with water	*con acqua*
wine	*vino*

THE MENU *(il menù)*

Ristorante and *trattorie* in holiday areas often have a tourist menu *(il menù turistico)*. This is usually a fixed price menu. It may look like good value but the quality of the food will depend very much on the restaurant owner's morals. There may be a children's menu too *(un menù per bambini* or *piatti per i bambini)*.

If you take a dictionary you'll probably manage to order from the 'real' menu with no trouble at all. Ask for the waiter's advice – see if the restaurant has any specialities *(le specialità della casa)* or try one of the specialities of the region *(le specialità regionali)*. If you're staying on the coast this is likely to be fish, seafood or some form of fish soup. In Tuscany you might be offered a tender Florentine T-bone steak, roast pork, beans and pasta in rich tomato sauce or even a bowl of tripe *(trippa)*! In the North the creamy *risotti* and rich *polente* baked with cheese and butter are not to be missed. You may be surprised to find frogs' legs *(cosce di rana)* on the menu in Piedmont – the French influence. In Rome and the Lazio look out for spit-roasted lamb *(abbacchio)* or kid *(capretto)* and slivers of tender artichoke *(carciofo)* in olive oil. In Emilia Romagna make sure you order a plate of local ham *(prosciutto)* and salami for the *antipasto*. The pizza was said to be invented in Naples. Whatever its history, it is certainly better here than anywhere else in the country. Try a *calzone* too – pizza that's been folded in half and fried or baked – very filling.

ANTIPASTO

A full meal starts with the *antipasto*. In large restaurants you'll be invited to make your own choice of cold meats *(affettati)*, shellfish salads *(frutti di mare)*, pimentoes or artichokes in oil and countless other mouthwatering possibilities. A smaller establishment may simply bring you whatever they have – slices of local salami perhaps, or *croûtons (crostini)* spread with delicate chicken liver pâté. In Tuscany they may produce a dish of uncooked broad beans *(fave)* in their pods to shell and eat with mature *pecorino* (sheep's cheese). Don't be like the English professor who visited some friends of ours and ate his way stolidly through the pods as well!

FIRST COURSE *(il primo)*

The main course *(il primo* or *minestra)* will be soup *(zuppa)*, pasta, or perhaps a *risotto* if you're in the North. The Italians don't use the sieve or liquidizer to nearly the same extent as we do and the soups tend to be chunky rather than smooth. Try the minestrone. Every cook has his or her own version and, eaten with a sprinkling of parmesan and some good crusty bread there's nothing quite like it. Every region favours different shapes of pasta to eat with its own pasta sauces. In Genoa they serve *trenette*, thin, match-stick strips of pasta, with *pesto* sauce (made of basil). You can get *pesto* all over Italy during the summer, but there's nothing quite like the one made from basil grown on the balmy Ligurian coast.

MAIN COURSE *(il secondo)*

The main course is usually meat *(carne)* or fish *(pesce)*. If you're vegetarian it's best to be diplomatic. Vegetarianism has become more common in Italy over the last ten years and many of the larger cities have vegetarian restaurants. However, if you find yourself in an ordinary restaurant, take the advice of an ex-vegetarian and say that you just don't feel like eating meat or fish today. Even the crustiest old waiter will rise to the challenge of finding you an alternative, while the very word 'vegetarian' *(vegetariano)* will simply antagonize him! There's nothing to stop you leaving out the main course all together. There's never any obligation to order all the courses – even the Italians with their mythical appetites don't feel like eating four or five courses every time they go to a restaurant.

VEGETABLES *(i contorno)*

There will be a choice of vegetables to go with the main course. These will be served on separate plates which are often brought to the table after the meat or fish. If you have fried potatoes (*patate fritte*) they should be piping hot. Otherwise, don't be surprised if all of your main course is on the tepid side. The Italians don't share our obsession with hot food – perhaps because the climate is so much warmer.

You will generally be offered the choice of a green salad (*insalata verde*) or a mixed one (*insalata mista*). There will be oil, vinegar and salt on the table for you to pour on to it.

DESSERTS (*i dessert*)

The choice of desserts will again depend on the size of the restaurant or *trattoria*. In a restaurant there may be a trolley or a side table with a display of fresh fruit (*frutta*) and creamy, calorific puddings. Caramel custard (*il creme caramel*) or *profiteroles* (*i bignè*) are standard fare at tourist restaurants. Other places may offer rich *zabaglione* made from Marsala whipped up with eggs (see MENUS AND RECIPES), caramelized oranges (*arancie caramellate*), fruit salad (*macedonia*), rich home-made ice-cream (*i gelati*) or refreshing water ices (*granite*). If you choose to eat fruit you'll often be brought a bowl of water and a knife and fork. The water is for rinsing it in and the knife and fork are to be used for the delicate operation of peeling and consuming. You'll be get a knife and fork for your cheese (*formaggio*) too. This is a good opportunity to taste the local cheeses – ask for *un formaggio della regione*.

You'll be offered coffee at the end of the meal. *Un espresso* is the traditional thing to have. You'll never see an Italian drinking *cappuccino* to round off the meal – strictly a breakfast or mid-morning drink.

THE BILL (*il conto*)

When your bill arrives it will include a payment for *pane e coperto* – the bread and a cover charge. If service is included it will be itemized as well. If there's no mention of a service charge (*servizio*) it's customary to tip the waiter 10%. You'll be given a receipt (*ricevuta*). A recent law, designed to prevent tax evasion, requires you to take this with you. Don't leave it on the table or you'll have the waiter chasing you down the street with it!

If you plan to pay by credit card, make sure that the relevant sticker is on display in the window before you go in. If you leave the tourist trail you're unlikely to be able to use travellers cheques – ask about it before sitting down.

You'll find that children are welcome in restaurants and *trattorie* at lunchtime or in the evening (see Chapter 9, CHILDREN AND BABIES).

USEFUL WORDS AND PHRASES

Can we see the menu please?	*Vorremmo vedere il menù?*
Can we eat outside?	*Possiamo mangiare all'aperto?*
Could we see the menu again?	*Vorremmo vedere di nuovo il menù?*
Could we have the bill please.	*Il conto per favore.*
Could we have some of the house wine please?	*Ci può portare del vino della casa per piacere?*
I'm not allowed to eat. . .	*Io non posso mangiare. . .*
Is there a speciality of the house/the region?	*Avete una specialità della casa/della regione?*
Is there a toilet please?	*C'è un bagno per favore?*
Is there a tourist menu?	*Avete un menù thristico?*
May we have more bread/water/wine, please?	*Ci porta ancora del pane/dell'acqua/del vino, per favore?*
What do you recommend?	*Cosa ci consiglia di mangiare?*
waiter	*il cameriere*
waitress	*la cameriera*
baked	*al forno*
boiled	*lesso*
cheese	*il formaggio*
dish of the day	*il piatto del giorno*
first course	*il primo*
fish	*il pesce*
fried	*fritto*

fruit	*la frutta*
fruit salad	*la macedonia di frutta*
green salad	*l'insalata verde*
grilled	*ai ferri/alla griglia*
meat	*la carne*
mixed salad	*l'insalata mista*
oil	*l'olio*
on a skewer	*allo spiedo*
pepper	*il pepe*
roast	*arrosto*
salad	*l'insalata*
salt	*il sale*
seafood	*i frutti di mare*
second course	*il secondo*
smoked	*affumicato*
soup	*la zuppa, la minestra*
stewed	*in umido*
stuffed	*ripieno*
vegetables	*le verdure, il contorno*
vinegar	*l'aceto*
water ice	*la granita*

CHAPTER SEVEN

SHOPPING FOR FOOD

The Italians don't seem to favour the English tradition of the 'weekly shop'. They do their shopping daily, demanding, and usually finding, extremely fresh ingredients. Don't waste any time in finding out what cheeses, wines, fruits, vegetables, hams and sausages are local to your area – they are bound to be the freshest, tastiest ingredients to be had. Frozen and convenience foods can be bought but there is still very little demand for foods out of season. Should you decide to eat like the locals you will find that your recipes are not only regional but seasonal too. Take advantage of the abundance of fruit and vegetables that we think of as luxuries in our own country. What's the point of making a dessert every day when you can feast off really fresh figs, peaches, watermelons or muscat grapes?

There is a ritual and an expertise attached to shopping for food in Italy that elevates it from being a chore to something of an art. Give yourself plenty of time and you'll find that buying the groceries can become one of the great pleasures of your Italian holiday.

THE MARKET (il mercato)

The open-air market is the best place to buy fruit and vegetables – it's here that the cheapest and freshest ones are to be found. When you get to your holiday apartment or house ask the neighbours when and where the market is: Where is the market? *Dov'è il mercato?* Is there a market today? *Oggi è giornata di mercato?*

Market shopping in Italy is a delight that never wanes. Italians seem to have an inherent aesthetic sense – even on the busiest market stall the fruit and vegetables will be arranged to delight the eye. Go in the early morning and enjoy the beautiful scents and colours at their best. If you have to go later in the day prepare yourselves for a bit of jostling. It's often quite noisy too – a good excuse for performing your deals in sign-language if you can't muster the words! Most towns and cities have an open market once a week. Don't expect to be able to bargain for food. This may be appropriate if you're shopping for clothes or shoes, but food prices are always fixed. If you're prepared to hang around, some stalls may cut their prices at the end of the day.

In larger towns and cities there is nearly always a permanent, covered food market. This is often a good place to buy meat and cheese. Prices are often lower than those in the ordinary shops.

HE SHOP (*il negozio*)

You'll find all the usual shops, although some of them do things slightly differently from their counterparts in Britain. For example, there are two shops that do what our baker does, the *panificio* (baker), which sells breads, pizza slices, pizza dough and biscuits, and the *pasticceria* (pastry shop), which sells cakes and sweetmeats of all sorts. Meat is sold both by the butcher (*macelleria*) and the poulterer (*pollaiolo*). There is also the delicatessen (*salumeria*) which sells cured meats, and the *rosticceria* (cooked meat stall). Fruit and vegetables can be bought either at the market or the greengrocer's (*fruttivendolo*). Tinned food is bought either from the supermarket (*supermercato*) or the grocer's (*alimentari*). Dairy products are bought at the *latteria* (dairy), although cheese is also sold in the *latteria* (dairy and cheese shop), as

101

well as by the *salumeria*. Fish is bought at the *pescheria* (fishmonger).

Many of the larger shops now use a ticket queueing system. The ticket dispenser is usually near the door. Take your ticket and then wait for your number to come up. Be fearless about shouting and waving your ticket when it does – you won't get a second chance if you miss your turn. It's quite common to find yourself being served by one person and then paying another at the till. Occasionally there is a third person to wrap your goods. The careful and often decorative wrapping that they go in for in Italy has the effect of imbuing your purchases with quality and importance.

OPENING TIMES

Food shops generally open at eight o'clock each morning. In villages, towns and even the smaller cities they close for lunch at one. During the summer they open again from four until eight. In winter afternoon opening is usually from three until seven. Wednesday is a half day in the winter in some parts of Italy, but in summer shops stay open all day on Wednesday and close on Saturday afternoons. Large supermarkets tend to open a bit later than the smaller shops, but then they stay open all day without closing for lunch.

USEFUL WORDS AND PHRASES

I would like. . .	*Vorrei. . .*
large/larger	*grande/più grande*
small/smaller	*piccolo/più piccolo*
this/that	*questo/quello*
Where can I buy. . .?	*Dove posso comprare. . .?*
a bit more/less	*un po' di più/meno*
a bottle of. . .	*una bottiglia di. . .*
a box of. . .	*una scatola di*
a litre of/half litre of	*un litro di/un mezzo litro di*
Give me half a kilo of . . . please	*Mi dia mezzo chilo di . . . per favore*

Give me half of it please	*Mi ne dia la metà, per favore*
How much does it cost?	*Quanto costa?*
How much does a kilo cost?	*Quanto costa un chilo?* or *Quant'è al chilo?*
Is it fresh?	*E fresco?*
Is it ripe?	*E maturo?*
Is there a bigger/smaller one?	*Ce n'è uno più grande/piccolo?*
a kilo (2.2lbs)	*un chilo*
100g (approx 4oz)	*un etto*
50g (approx 2oz)	*cinquanta grammi/un mezz'etto*

BREAD (pane)

Bread is sold by the kilo and large loaves are cut up as necessary. Don't buy too much at a time as most of it goes stale quite quickly.

Bread is nearly always eaten with meals, taking the place of a knife to push the food onto the fork and used for mopping up sauces and gravies at the end of the meal. At restaurants a basket of bread, rolls or bread sticks is always put onto the table the moment you arrive. Beware of eating it all before you start the meal!

The average village shop doesn't offer much of a choice of breads. You'll probably only be able to buy the local *pane casareccio* or *pancarrè* – a sort of long-life sliced loaf only really suitable for toast and toasted sandwiches. On the other hand, sophisticated city bakers offer a wide variety. Sometimes they even make German or Austrian rye breads (*pane di segale*) as well as regional breads from all over the country.

Bread varies dramatically from region to region. The Tuscan variety is unsalted, scarcely leavened and cooked in a wood fired oven. In Sardinia they eat sheets of crisp, unleavened bread called *carta da musica* ('music paper' or 'score sheets'). The northern Italian breads, by contrast, are often airy and insubstantial. If you want a simple white loaf ask for *pane casareccio*. It's usually round or oval with a coarse texture and a thick crust to it.

Some breads that are made all over Italy go by different names in the different regions. For example, the hollow white rolls known as *rosette* in central and southern Italy are called *michette* in the North. Some loaves contain olives (*pane con olive*), some are made with the addition of olive oil and others with milk. In some areas there are special loaves that only appear for particular festivals and saints' days. In Siena they make *pan co' santi* (bread with saints) for All Saints' Day. This is a delicious circular fruit loaf with walnuts in it. The currants and raisins are supposed to represent the saints!

Large bakers sell their own biscuits, pizza slices and lumps of dough that you can take home to make pizzas yourself. You'll often see huge, rectangular trays of pizza being taken out of the oven and cut up with scissors. It's sold by weight - choose a slice to suit your appetite! Another delicious snack is *focaccia* - a crisp, unleavened dough base that's been sprinkled with coarse salt and sometimes baked with the addition of fresh rosemary or onions. Some bakers make fresh pasta (*pasta fresca*).

CAKES AND PASTRIES (*torte e paste*)

The *pasticceria* (pastry shop) is devoted solely to the production and sale of cakes and pastries. Even the smallest Italian towns and villages seem to have their own special cakes and sweets. I hope that you'll seek out the local specialities and take them home to try out. Most *pasticcerie* sell glazed fruit tarts (*crostate di frutta*) in addition to the local specialities. If there is a cold cabinet in the shop it means that they also have chilled puddings (*semifreddi*). These generally consist of a mixture of cream and chocolate or fruit. Generally speaking, you can go to a *pasticceria* anywhere in the country and find the tiny, sweet and decorative biscuits that are known as *biscottini*. They are sold by the *etto* (100g/4oz), and eaten with coffee or sometimes even with an aperitif. *Torrone* is a rich white nougat sold fresh in *pasticcerie* all over Italy. It's often coated in a thick layer of chocolate. *Amaretti* or macaroons were invented by the Italians. The best known are *amaretti di Saronno*, but you'll find slightly different sorts all over the country.

Pasta frolla, a kind of enriched shortcrust pastry, and *pasta sfoglia* (flaky pastry) are used as the basis for several famous sweetmeats. Neapolitan *sfogliatella* is made out of *pasta sfoglia* shaped into a fan and filled with *ricotta*, chocolate and candied fruit. *Ricotta* – a soft ewe's milk cheese – is often used in puddings. In MENUS AND RECIPES I have avoided desserts that involve pastry making and opted for the simpler and less time-consuming *ricotta* and fruit-based recipes.

In Sicily *pasta reale* (marzipan) is used to make magnificent imitation fruits and tiny iced cakes. In Siena *panforte*, made with nuts, dried fruit and honey, is often eaten with a glass of good Chianti. Sienese *copate*, little honey wafers, and the almond biscuits known as *ricciarelli* are delicious too. In Friuli the cakes are more Austrian than Italian, with strudels, fritters and sweet tarts.

Some sweets and cakes only appear on saints' days or during the carnival season. In Perugia they eat a special macaroon made from pine nuts at Christmas. The Milanese Christmas *panettone*, a light golden sponge sprinkled with icing sugar, has become the traditional Christmas cake all over the country.

GROCERIES (*generi alimentari*)

There are some things that you'll probably want to buy as soon as you get to your holiday home. The typical Italian storecupboard contains a few basic ingredients which can be found in the grocer (*negozio de generi alimentari*) or supermarket (*supermercato*). You can often buy dried and tinned goods at the greengrocer's (*fruttivendolo*). You'll find tinned tomatoes here (*pomodori pelati*), white and red haricot beans, chick peas and dried mushrooms (*fagiolini*, *borlotti*, *ceci* and *funghi secchi*).

Breakfast **cereals** (*cereali*) are something of an eccentric luxury in Italy. However, as they are often part of the English family's staple diet, they've found their place in this otherwise very Italian list. Cereals usually cost the earth and you can't always get them at an ordinary grocer – although supermarkets usually have them. Strangely, some chemists (*farmacia*) sell cornflakes – proof that they are looked on as part of a 'special diet'!

Capers (*capperi*) are conserved in salt or vinegar. Some places sell them loose out of a huge, salt encrusted tub. If they're very salty you should soak them in fresh water for an hour or two. Coffee (*caffè*) is usually very finely ground for the *espresso* machine or *caffettiera*. Nescafé can be bought virtually everywhere and so can decaffinated Café Hag (most bars will make you a decaffinated *espresso* – ask for *un'Hag*). Orzoro, made from roasted barley, is another caffeine-free drink but it's a bit of an acquired taste. You can make it in the same way as *espresso*.

Flour (*farina*) is made from all kinds of things in Italy – chestnuts, maize, potatoes and rice to name but a few. Farina 00 or *farina di grano duro* is wheatflour, the only sort for making pastry as we know it. For cakes buy *farina di grano tenero*. This is a soft, plain flour. You can't buy self-raising flour in Italy so get some baking powder as well. For cakes you'll need *lievito per dolci*. If you want to make bread or pizza you'll need yeast (*lievito per pane* or *lievito per pizza/di birra*).

Nuts (*noci*) can be bought at the *fruttivendolo*. Common varieties available are: almonds (*mandorle*), chestnuts (*castagne*), hazelnuts (*nocciole*), pine kernels (*pinoli*) and walnuts (*noci*).

Olives (*olive*) can be divided into the cheaper, shrivelled-looking varieties used for cooking, and the larger, plumper ones, usually from Puglia, for eating. The latter are usually stored in trays or tubs at the delicatessen or the market. They come stored in brine or oil, and are often marinated in herbs or stuffed.

Olive oil (*olio d'oliva*), is a vital ingredient in Italian cooking. It is used less in the North than in central and southern Italy. This is due to the simple fact that olive trees grow more successfully further south and consequently in the north of Italy butter, or a mixture of oil and butter, has become the traditional medium for cooking. The very best quality oil is called *olio d'oliva extra vergine*. This means that it is obtained from the first pressing of the olives. You'll find virgin oil quite expensive. It's too good for ordinary cooking – use it for drizzling over salads, mild cheeses like Mozzarella, Ricotta or Stracchino. After the olive harvest people often make *bruschetta* with the first of the virgin oil. This is simply slices of toasted – preferably Tuscan – bread rubbed with fresh garlic, sprinkled with salt and then drizzled with the fresh virgin oil. *Olio d'oliva vergine* is made from the second pressing of the olives. It's slightly cheaper but still very good. Plain *olio d'oliva* can be made at any time during successive pressings. Vegetable oil, which is fine for frying, is often made from maize and called *olio di mais*.

Pasta is probably the most important single ingredient in the Italian diet. You can either buy the dried, industrially produced sort, or treat yourself to fresh pasta (*pasta fresca*) on the day that you plan to eat it. The shape of pasta that you choose should depend on the type of sauce you plan to serve with it. Traditionally shellfish sauces are served with fine spaghetti, hollow shells and tubes with meat sauces, and creamy sauces with ribbon pasta such as *tagliatelle*. Most pasta is made from plain durum wheat flour (*semola di grano duro*). Some has spinach added to it to make it green or tomato to turn it pink. Pasta *all'uovo* contains eggs and is usually used for making *tagliatelle* or *fettuccine*.

If you're using dried pasta you should allow about 100g (4oz) per person. Bakers often sell fresh, stuffed pasta such as *tortellini* and *ravioli*. Allow 150g (5oz) of this per person. Not just because they're so good – they weigh more too! You can buy *ravioli* vacuum packed, frozen or dried. Naturally, it's not nearly as good as the freshly made stuff. When you cook dried pasta you should allow 4 litres (7 pints) of water to half a kilo (1lb) of pasta. Bring the water to a rolling boil, add a tablespoon of salt and add the pasta. Stir well to prevent sticking and return to the pan to do some more stirring throughout the cooking time. Boil uncovered for about 12 minutes, but start testing it after ten. There's nothing worse – and nothing more comically English in Italian eyes – than overcooking the pasta.

Fresh pasta cooks very quickly. With stuffed varieties it's best to cook a few at a time. They take about five minutes, but start testing as soon as the pieces bob to the surface.

There is an enormous variety of different types of pasta, often used for different sorts of dishes. Taking them in alphabetical order they are: *agnolini* (small *ravioli*), *bucatini* (thick, hollow spaghetti), *cannelloni* (large tubes for stuffing), *conchiglie* (shell-shaped), *farfalle* (butterflies), *fettuccine* (ribbon pasta made with eggs), *fusilli* (spirals), *lasagne* (wide strips of egg pasta for baked dishes), *maccheroni* (small tubes), *pappardelle* (broad ribbon pasta with a fluted edge), *penne* (quills), *ravioli* (pasta squares often stuffed with *ricotta* and spinach), *rigatoni* (ridged tubes for baked dishes), *tortellini* (shape often compared to a belly button; they're usually stuffed with minced meat), *trenette* (thin, match-like strips), *vermicelli* (very fine spaghetti, often cooked in broth).

In addition to the larger varities of pasta there are any number of tiny pasta shapes to be used in soups and broths. You can even buy specially manufactured pasta for babies!

Rice (*riso*) In Lombardy and the North rice tends to be used more than pasta. The *arborio* rice that grows in the Po Valley is ideal for *risotto* – a vital element in northern regional cookery. Use it yourself and you'll find that you can make a perfect *risotto* with the greatest of ease. You can also use *riso vialone*. Both are round-grained varieties that produce the correct creamy texture with very little help from the cook.

Salt (*sale*) Unground sea salt is called *sale grosso marino*. Fine table salt is *sale fino da tavola*. **Sugar** (*zucchero*) is finer than our granulated sugar but not as fine as castor sugar. You can easily use it in place of castor sugar (*zucchero in polvere*), which can be a bit difficult to find.

Tinned **tomatoes** (*pomodori pelati*) are fundamental to Italian cooking. Tomato paste (*concentrato di pomodoro*) comes in a jar or a tube. You'll also find cardboard cartons of *passato*, which is puréed tomato sauce to which you need only to add the appropriate seasoning, (garlic, salt, pepper and some chopped herbs). **Vinegar** (*aceto*) can be red or white – it's always made from wine.

MILK, CHEESE AND EGGS *(latte, formaggio e uova)*

All the **milk** is homogenized in Italy. This means that the milk and cream are blended together to prevent the cream from separating. It tastes quite unlike English milk – as your children will probably tell you. I once heard of an expatriate English couple who, driven to despair by the poor quality of Italian milk, imported a Jersey cow to live with them in the Chianti. Sadly for them, the experiment proved that it's not only the breed of cow that determines the quality of the milk. After a good feed of Mediterranean grass their cow was producing just the same milk as her Italian counterparts.

You can buy fresh milk (*latte fresco*) from the dairy (*latteria*), the supermarket and most grocers. In some cities cartons of milk can be bought at bars. Whole milk is called *latte intero*, skimmed is *latte scremato* and partially skimmed is *parzialmente scremato*. UHT (*latte di lunga conservazione*) is easier to find than fresh.

Fresh cream (*panna fresca*) is very difficult to find. Ask at the *latteria* and try the supermarket – you may be lucky. The UHT cream used in cooking comes in a little box and is known as *panna da cucina*. Whipping cream, which usually has sugar folded into it after it's been whipped, is called *panna da montare*. It's used with glorious abundance on top of ice cream, cakes and fruit. Both types of UHT can be bought from grocers, supermarkets and *latterie*.

Yoghurt (*yogurt*) is as popular in Italy as it is in this country. It can be bought from supermarkets, grocers or *latterie*. Yomo and Danone are the best known brands. In the North they sell Alleluia which is especially creamy and calorific. Low fat yoghurts are labelled *magro*.

All Italian butter (*burro*) is unsalted. It can be bought from the *latteria*, supermarket or grocer, so can margerine (*margarina*).

Cheese (*formaggio*) is made all over Italy on a local basis and each area has its own speciality. Buying fresh, local cheeses is one of the joys of travelling in Italy. Go to the cheese stall at the food market, the *latteria*, the delicatessen (*salumeria*) or the *casa del formaggio* if there is one. If you can't see any, ask if they have a local cheese: *Avete qualche formaggio nostrano?* It's usually made from a mixture of cow's and sheep's or goat's milk. In the South buffalo milk is also used, although most of it goes into making Mozzarella. Some of these cheeses are now produced on an industrial scale and sold all over Italy; Invernizzi is one of the largest manufacturers.

Look out for farms that sell their cheese direct. In the South Mozzarella is sometimes sold in this way. Look out for signs on the roadside and follow them for an experience that you'll never forget – really fresh *mozzarella di bufala* is indescribably delicious.

Cow's milk cheeses (vacchini) Those listed here are the more common varieties. I've listed them alphabetically. Asiago is a northern Italian cheese. It comes from the mountainous area of the Veneto and is made from partially skimmed cow's milk. You'll find that you can get it fresh – which is cheapest – slightly matured (*mezzano*) or fully mature (*stravecchio*), when it becomes a good grating cheese. Bel Paese, a soft, mild cheese, is probably the most commonly exported of all Italian cheeses, while Dolcelatte is a soft blue cheese. Fontina is a mountain cheese from Piedmont in the North of the country. It's a good melting cheese – ideal for fondue – with a strong, almost sweet taste. Gorgonzola is made in Lombardy. It's a strong, creamy, blue-veined cheese, ideal for melting and for eating as it is.

Mascarpone is a thick, fresh cream cheese that serves as the basis for several delicious puddings. Make sure you keep it in the fridge and eat it before it can go off. Mozzarella '*fior di latte*' is a cow's milk Mozzarella. Not nearly as good as the traditional, buffalo milk version, but cheaper and more readily available, it's ideal for cooking – there's no point in paying more for something that you're going to melt and cover in herbs. Keep it in the fridge, covered with water and milk.

Parmigiano (parmesan) is also known as Grana Padana. Genuine parmesan has the words *Parmigiano–Reggiano* etched onto the rind – delicious eaten on its own or with a hunk of bread and a glass of good red wine. Parmesan is perhaps the most extensively used ingredient in Italian cooking. It's usually aged before it's sold, and will keep indefinitely in the fridge as long as you don't let it dry out. Put it into a sealed plastic box or wrap it well in a plastic bag. Try to avoid buying it ready grated – you can never be sure what's gone into it.

Robbiola is a creamy, soft cheese from Lombardy, while Stracchino is a soft, creamy cheese that's very popular with children. It has a mild taste that marries well with a little olive oil and black pepper – eat it with a fork or on a slice of bread. Svizzero is simply Emmental, which is very popular in Italy. The Italians make their own version of Gruyère, known as Groviera. Taleggio is a runny cheese from Lombardy. Taleggino is the mature version of the same thing.

Sheep's milk cheeses (pecorino) Pecorino is the most important of the ewe's milk cheeses. It's generally made in Tuscany and Sardinia. When fresh (*pecorino fresco*) it's a mild, quite creamy cheese in an orange rind. The mature cheese (*pecorino stagionato*) is darker, drier and powerfully flavoured. At this stage it becomes a good grating cheese. The Sardinian variety (*pecorino sardo*) is often used in place of parmesan.

Ricotta is a soft, white cheese made from ewe's milk from the area around Rome. It's unsalted and makes the ideal base for sauces and puddings. Try it with sugar and a pinch of cinnamon or with nothing but a sprinkling of salt. A spoonful of Ricotta in a tomato pasta sauce will make it deliciously creamy.

Buffalo's milk cheeses (formaggi di latte di bufala) Buffalo milk cheeses are the products of the South – the buffaloes themselves are worth seeing and their cheeses are some of the best in the country. Mozzarella *di bufala* is a leavened buffalo milk cheese. It's made in the provinces of Campania, Puglia and Calabria. If you're staying in the South you'll probably find the fresh Mozzarella so good that you won't want to eat anything else. Some of it's plaited and called *treccia*, and some is made into creamy, bite-sized pieces or *bocconcini*. It all has a delicious and delicate flavour that makes it perfect on its own or sliced into a salad. You should try to eat Mozzarella absolutely fresh. It's stored in a buttermilk bath in the shop; make sure it doesn't dry out before you eat it.

Provola and Provolone are made in Campania. Provola is a small, pear-shaped cheese with a yellow rind. It is often smoked which gives it a deeper colour and a rich, smoky flavour. Provolone is an enormous, sausage shaped cheese which can be made from cow's or buffalo's milk. It's usually sold slightly mature and has a strong, tangy flavour. There's a new, smaller type of Provolone called Provolino.

USEFUL WORDS

affumicato	smoked
caprino	made from goat's milk

dolce	sweet
mezzano	slightly mature
nostrano	local
piccante	sharp
stagionato	mature
stravecchio	very mature and strong

Eggs (*uova*) can generally be bought from the grocer (*generi alimentari*), the poulterer (*pollaiolo*) or the super-market. They used to be sold in pairs. If you wanted half a dozen you'd ask for *tre coppie* and take them home in a paper bag or, at best, wrapped in newspaper. But that was a long time ago. The egg box has become almost universal in the last ten years but you may still find them being sold loose at the village shop.

FRUIT AND VEGETABLES *(frutta e verdura)*

There's something thrilling about transforming luxurious Mediterranean fruit and vegetables into your staple diet. Even the more familiar ones taste completely different when they're really fresh – a fresh Sicilian orange will fill the house with scent when it's peeled. We are familiar with nearly all the Mediterranean fruits and vegetables in England now. There's not much that you won't recognize, so the items described here are included either because they're typically Italian, or because they're special in some way. There's a list of the common fruits and vegetables with the Italian names at the end of this section.

Tomatoes (*pomodori*) are a fundamental ingredient in recipes from the north to the south of the country. They are grown all over Italy and during the summer people make enough tomato sauce to last them through the year. However, a summer journey through the Campania would be enough to convince anyone that the South is the real heartland of tomato production. The roads are full of slow-moving, brightly painted open lorries, filled to overflowing with ripe plum tomatoes.

Autumn is the time for mushrooms (*funghi*) of every shape and size. After the first rain everybody seems to take to the woods. I know of one office that simply closes for a day's mushroom picking. There are over 3000 types of edible mushrooms in Italy, but the most common are *porcini* (our boletus) and *spugnole* (morels). Remember that mushrooms are priced by the kilo. Even if the price sounds high you'll get a lot for your money. *Porcini* are very rich too, so you won't need many of them to make a sustantial meal (see MENUS AND RECIPES, Chapter 8). Mushrooms are often sold either from a basket or the back of a three-wheeled truck parked at the edge of the market.

Truffle hunting is a more specialized affair. Truffles (*tartufi*) are something that we know very little about in this country. In Italy they grow underground beneath the oak trees of Umbria, Piedmont and Tuscany. It's said that truffle hunting is a matter of the utmost secrecy. The specially trained dogs are taken to the woods under the cover of dark – it's important that no one else should find out where the truffles come from. If you are in Italy during the autumn you should be able to buy some, albeit at enormous expense. You'll know that a shop sells fresh truffles the moment you open the door – the whole place will be filled with the scent of damp leaves. They are usually grated over fresh pasta, the Piedmontese version of fondue, and some white meat dishes.

Wild salad stuffs (*insalata da campo*) – such as purslane and arugula – often find their way to the market in the same informal way as mushrooms. Most of them are quite bitter and taste best in small quantities mixed in with other salad ingredients. Like spinach and other greens, salad stuff is usually bound together with rushes or pliable twigs, as it has been for hundreds of years. Fresh herbs (*erbe aromatiche*) are generally sold by the bunch (*un mazzo*).

There are some things that don't always appear on the stalls. In the spring look out for *contadini* (peasant farmers) selling long, thin spears of wild asparagus (*asparagi selvatici*) at the edge of the market.

Prickly pears (*fichi d'India*) might come as a surprise to some people. They are the fruit of the kind of cactuses that feature in westerns. Oval and covered in the sharpest and most penetrating of prickles, they start to arrive in the shops towards the end of the summer. Hold them down with a fork while you cut away the prickles to reveal the sweet, orange flesh. Sliced thinly and served with a squeeze of lemon juice they taste quite exotic.

If you find a good greengrocer (*fruttivendolo*), stick to it. Greengrocers are notoriously generous to their regular customers. You'll sometimes hear people asking the green-grocer for *un po' di odori*. They'll be given a bundle containing a stick of celery, a carrot and some parsley – the basis of a traditional tomato pasta sauce or a good soup. Regular customers aren't expected to pay for this. You can buy *odori* in the market too.

Spring and summer fruits and vegetables

apricots	*albicocche*
artichokes	*carciofi*
asparagus	*asparagi*
aubergines	*melanzane*
blackcurrants	*ribes*
broad beans	*fave*
broccoli	*broccoli*
cherries	*cigliegi*
chicory (white)	*cicoria*
chicory (red)	*radicchio or ravanello*
chilli pepper	*peperoncino*
courgettes	*zucchini*
cucumber	*cetriolo*
fennel	*finocchio*
figs	*fichi*
grapes	*uva*
lettuce	*lattuga*

mangetout	*piselli mangiatutto*
marrow	*zucca*
melon	*melone*
nectarines	*nocepesche*
peaches	*pesche*
plums	*prugne*
peas	*piselli*
peppers	*peperoni*
pomegranate	*melograno*
pineapple	*ananas*
raspberries	*lamponi*
strawberries	*fragole*
tomatoes (cooking)	*pomodori (da sugo)*
watermelon	*anguria or cocomero*

Autumn and winter fruits and vegetables

apples	*mele*
bananas	*banane*
beet or chard	*bietola or biete*
blackberries	*more*
cabbage (red)	*cavolo (rosso)*
savoy cabbage	*verza*
carrots	*carote*
cauliflower	*cavolfiore*
celery	*sedano*
grapefruit	*pompelmo*
leeks	*porri*
lemon	*limone*
mushrooms	*funghi*
onions	*cipolle*
oranges	*arance*
pears	*pere*
persimmons	*cachi*
potatoes	*patate*
spinach	*spinaci*

Herbs (odori)

basil	*basilico*

bay leaves	*alloro*
garlic	*aglio*
marjoram	*maggiorana*
mint	*menta*
oregano	*origano*
parsley	*prezzemolo*
rosemary	*rosmarino*
sage	*salvia*
tarragon	*dragoncello*
thyme	*timo*

Spices (spezie)

cinnamon	*cannella*
cloves	*chiodi di garofano*
saffron	*zafferano*
vanilla	*vaniglia*

POULTRY AND GAME *(pollame e caccia)*

Chicken is the cheapest meat. Chicken breast *(petto di pollo)* is very popular. It's sold ready boned and can be stuffed or opened out and fried as a tender escalope. The same goes for turkey *(petto di tacchino)*. You can usually buy free range chicken which is called *pollo a terra. Pollo nostrale* is local non-battery chicken – probably raised in a deep litter shed.

Rabbit *(coniglio)*, hare *(lepre)* and pigeon *(piccione)* are all popular and relatively cheap. A lot of people raise their own rabbits and in the country you'll often see bundles of grass being carried home to fatten the rabbit.

MEAT *(la carne)*

It's always a bit difficult buying meat in a foreign country. In Italy the cuts of meat vary from region to region and so do the words used to describe them, which complicates matters still further. Don't worry. All you need do is tell the butcher what you want to cook he'll give you the best meat for the job. Italians often buy their meat in this way too.

The amount of meat eaten in Italy varies from region to region. Generally speaking in the South, with its history of poverty and poor pastureland, meat is eaten rather less than in the North.

BEEF *(manzo)*

Tuscany, in the centre of Italy, is prime beef country. They eat a lot of meat here and the *bistecca alla fiorentina*, or Florentine T-bone steak, is one of the most important regional specialities. Should you order *bistecca alla fiorentina* in a restaurant, don't be surprised when they bring an enormous slab of raw meat to your table. It's not a dish for the faint-hearted. The idea is that you should run a practised eye over it and choose the size and cut of your very own steak. The meat will then be whisked away, cut up, cooked over charcoal embers and magically transformed into the tenderest and most succulent meat you've ever tasted. Tougher cuts of beef are usually stewed with red wine. If you want stewing steak ask the butcher for *spezzatino*.

Minced beef is sold principally for *ragù* (pasta sauce). Every region has its own version of *ragù*, but they all need long, slow cooking. The mince that goes into them must be really fresh or it might go off during the cooking process. Unlike our own butchers, the Italians only use the best quality meat for mincing. You'll probably be expected to choose your meat and then it will be minced for you.

Boiled beef (*bollito*) is a simple, cheap and popular meal. Technically, *un bollito* should contain a number of different meats, including beef, chicken, sausages, tongue and sometimes a calf's head as well! However, for a cheap, nourishing supper ask the butcher for *bollito* and he'll give you a collection of beef bones and meat scraps. If you tell him how many people you're planning to feed (*bollito per . . . persone*) he'll be able to give you the right amount. All you have to do is boil the meat and stock bones very slowly in water with a few potatoes or carrots. When it's cooked the meat should be served with *salsa verde* (green sauce). This is made by chopping a few capers, an anchovy, a little onion, half a clove of garlic and a good handful of parsley. Mix the finely chopped ingredients with enough olive oil and lemon juice to make a pouring sauce. The left-over meat stock will give you the basis for a lovely, rich soup.

Veal (*vitello*) tends to be eaten rather more than beef in other areas of the country. Veal escalopes (*scaloppine*) are cut very, very thin, flattened with a meat mallet and then fried for a couple of minutes on each side in butter or oil. A splash of white wine is often added at the end to create a rich gravy. Some of the most famous Italian meat dishes are made from veal. *Saltimbocca* is made from veal escalopes that are fried gently with slices of raw ham and fresh sage (see MENUS AND RECIPES). *Ossobuco*, another world famous dish, is made from the braised shin of the veal calf. The marrow inside the shin bone is considered a great delicacy.

LAMB *(agnello)*

Lamb is widely available in the familiar cuts. If you are staying in Rome or the Lazio in spring you'll probably come across tiny lambs and kids *(capretto)* on sale for roasting. Their tender, milk-fed meat in the dish called *abbacchio* i considered a great delicacy.

PORK *(maiale)*

In rural areas it's common to fatten your own pig. After it' slaughtered everyone works flat out to cure and preserve the meat. Fresh pork is generally considered a rather heavy meat more suitable for hearty winter meals than anything else. Chops are often grilled over charcoal or cooked in a rich tomato sauce. In Florence saddle of pork baked slowly with fresh rosemary and garlic is called *arista*. You'll often see *porchetta* being sold from roadside stalls and at fêtes and festivals all over Italy. It's sometimes sold by the butcher, the *rosticceria* (cooked meat stall) and the delicatessen as well. Thick slices of pork are cut from a whole, spit roasted pig, weighed and then handed to you between hunks of crusty white bread. The meat is usually very salty and highly seasoned with rosemary and garlic. The *rosticceria* nearly always sells wine by the glass as well – the combination i perfectly delicious.

Bacon *(pancetta)* is fattier than ours. It's usually diced and combined with other ingredients – such as parmesan and cream in *pasta alla carbonara* or tomatoes and peppers in *pasta alla matriciana*. *Guanciale* is bacon cut from the cheek rather than the belly. It can be smoked *(affumicato)* or unsmoked.

CURED AND PRESERVED MEATS *(salami)*

Butchers often stock cured meats as well as fresh and most grocers have at least a limited selection.

The ropes of semi-dried sausages *(luganega)* that hang from

the ceiling in butchers and grocers contain lots of pepper and sometimes chilli as well. Long slow cooking with tomatoes makes a rich, spicy sauce for pasta or *polenta*. Most butchers make their own fresh sausages (*salsiccia*). These tend to be rather fattier than our own, with coarser meat. Mortadella is a gigantic, cooked pork sausage that is sold in thin slices like salami. Some people find it a bit too fatty, but it's a good picnic standby.

There are numerous different varieties of salami. As always, each region has its own specialities. If you're not sure what they are ask for *un salame nostrano* (locally produced salami). In the North salamis are usually seasoned with peppercorns and in the South they often have tomatoes and spices in them as well.

Ham is either cooked (*prosciutto cotto*) or raw (*prosciutto crudo*). The raw hams are dried, cured with salt and then sliced paper thin. It's only the *prosciutto crudo* produced from pigs fed on the whey left over from making parmesan cheese that's called Parma ham. Other cured hams taste very much the same and tend to cost a little bit less. Try eating them on their own with a squeeze of lemon juice or accompanied by figs, melon or pears. *Speck* is smoked ham – it's often used as a garnish on pizzas.

Cured beef is called *bresaola*. Like Parma ham, it is sold in very thin slices. Eat it with a drizzle of good olive oil and some freshly ground black pepper as an *antipasto*.

The Italians are very good at finding uses for parts of the carcass that we usually prefer to forget. Florentine tripe sellers with their glass sided barrows are a testimony to this skill. Calves' heads, offal, pigs' trotters, brains and sweetbreads all have their place in the Italian kitchen.

USEFUL WORDS AND PHRASES

chop	*braciola*
cooked ham	*prosciutto cotto*
cutlet	*costoletta*
entrecote	*contra filetto*

escalope	*scaloppina*
fillet	*filetto*
kidney	*rognone*
liver	*fegato*
mince	*macinata*
ox tail	*coda alla vaccinara*
pheasant	*faggiano*
raw ham	*prosciutto crudo*
slice	*fettina*
steak	*bistecca*
stewing steak	*spezzatino*
A slice of that one please	*una fetta di quello per favore*

FISH *(pesce)*

On the whole the Italians eat far more fish than we do – particularly on the coasts and near the great lakes of the North. The varieties of fish vary from place to place. Even if you manage to learn their names in Italian you'll often find that there's a completely different dialect word for the same fish in every region. When you go to the fish market you may well find that you don't recognize what's on offer. Don't worry if you don't know exactly what you're buying. Really fresh fish has no need of elaborate sauces or garnishes. Most Mediterranean fish tastes delicious if you simply score the sides, brush it with oil and bake it in the oven. Serve it hot and crisp with a squeeze of lemon juice. Better still, cook it over hot charcoal embers, and eat it with crusty bread and a green salad.

It's hardly surprising that fish should be such an important ingredient in coastal areas. Each little port has its own, unique recipe for fish soup. Originally the soups that are now labelled as 'specialities' were simply a good way of using up fish that were too small to sell. In the Veneto there are some delightful recipes for red and grey mullet, squid, mussels and scampi.

Fishermen on the warmer waters of the southern coasts – Sicily and Sardinia – catch swordfish (*pesce spada*), sardines (*sarde*), shellfish (*frutti di mare*) and tuna (*tonno*). Again, these are the main ingredient in many delicious recipes.

The fish market near the Rialto in Venice is probably one of the most famous in the world. It's a magnificent place where the baskets of brightly coloured fresh fish glint in the early morning light. Mind you, it isn't a place for the squeamish or the would-be vegetarian. Be ready to avert your eyes if you can't stomach the sight of sea eels squirming as they are cut into manageable lengths or the hopeless pulsating of shellfish.

You can usually buy fresh fish wherever there are fishing boats. Don't automatically expect this to be the case on islands. Some island communities have traditionally ignored the sea to concentrate on farming – and they're not going to change their habits to accommodate a few tourists.

The fishmonger (*pescheria*) will be quite happy to gut your fish before you take it home. If you are planning to make a fish soup, make sure you take the heads home for the stock (see USEFUL PHRASES below). Large fish such as the gigantic tuna and the swordfish are sold in thick slices or steaks. These taste best grilled or barbecued.

If you're staying inland and away from any large rivers or lakes the fish will always be frozen. The Findus empire extends to Italy and includes a 'gourmet line' of fish soup (*zuppa di pesce*), and fish *risotto* (*risotto alla pescatore*). Findus fish fingers (*bastoncini di pesce*) are on sale at most supermarkets too.

Tuna and anchovies (*acciughe*) can be bought in tins or out of great, oily tubs at the grocer's. Strips of salt cod (*baccalà*) are sold by grocers all over the country too. Remember to soak it in cold water for at least twelve hours before you use it, to remove the salt.

USEFUL WORDS AND PHRASES

I'd like a fish suitable for baking please	*Vorrei un pesce per cucinare al forno per favore*
Please can you clean it for me?	*Me li pulisce per favore?*
Please can I take the heads to make stock	*Mi può dare le teste per fare il brodo?*
Please could you cut their heads off?	*può togliere le teste per favore?*
This is too big/small	*Questo è troppo grande/piccolo*
What's this one called?	*Come si chiama questo?*

Remember that dialect names – not included in this list – are often used.

anchovies	*acciughe/alici*
angler or monkfish	*rana pescatrice*
bream	*dentice/orata/sarago*
brill	*rombo liscio*
cod	*merluzzo*
dentex	*dentice*
eel	*anguilla/morena*
fish soup	*zuppa di pesce*
grey mullet	*cefalo/muggine*
grouper	*cernia*
John Dory	*pesce San Pietro*
red mullet	*triglia*
sea bass	*spigola*
sea bream	*orata*
skate	*razza*
sole	*sogliola*
sturgeon	*storione*
trout	*trota*

SHELLFISH *(frutti di mare)*

Shellfish is tremendously popular. Restaurants all around the coast serve fragrant bowls of piping hot mussel soup, pasta with tomato and clam sauce and seafood salads containing a wealth of clams *(vongole)* mussels *(cozze)*, squid *(calamari)* and prawns *(gamberi)*. (Ready-made seafood sauce for pasta or rice can be bought at supermarkets all over the country.) Shellfish are nearly always alive on the market stall and you'll often meet some quite active specimens in restaurants too. For some people prising open a live, uncooked clam and popping it straight into their mouths is one of life's pure delights!

USEFUL WORDS

crab	*granchio*
lobster	*aragosto*
octopus	*polipo*
oysters	*ostriche*
scallops	*canestrelli*
shrimps	*gamberetti*

WINE AND DRINKS *(vino e bevande)*

Wine is a vital ingredient in many Italian recipes. Anyone accustomed to cooking in our own country will experience an enormous sense of liberation as they splash a glass or two into the pan. Marsala, a sweet Sicilian dessert wine, also makes freqent appearances in recipes for meat, fish and desserts. Local wine, cheap blended table wines, liqueurs and Italian spirits can usually be bought from the grocer. Larger towns and cities will have a wine merchant *(enoteca)* where you can buy wines from all over the country.

CHAPTER EIGHT

MENUS AND RECIPES

You'll almost certainly want to try the local produce and regional dishes. However, if you're not familiar with the area, it can be difficult to find out what's on offer. Even when you do stumble across something you like, what ingredients do you need? What other dishes go well with it? And how long does it take to prepare? Even the most enthusiastic self-caterers don't want to spend hours and hours in the kitchen – after all, this is a holiday!

The menus and recipes given here vary from the quick-and-simple to those with the more adventurous cook in mind, and the ingredients are easily obtainable. Some menus take into account that there will be evenings when no one feels like cooking and feature dishes which, while being distinctively Italian, can be bought at a supermarket, grocer's or pastry shop, and require almost no preparation. The ingredients are listed with their Italian translations and some of the common brand names, so that you know what to ask for or look for when you shop. Where the ingredient is something you will be buying specifically for the dish, such as '600g (1lb 5oz) sardines' it is translated precisely, including quantities '*seicento grammi di sarde*'. However, where the item is something you are likely to buy anyway, only its name is translated – so '1 garlic clove, finely chopped' is simply translated as '*aglio*' (garlic).

NOTE ON MEASUREMENTS

Some of the recipes use a cup measurement, which you can take to be teacup-sized – containing between one third and one half a pint. The metric measurements are converted into imperial, but as a rough guide, 1 kilogram = just over 2lb, while 100 grams = about 4oz. With fluid measurements, 20fl oz = 1 pint, and 1 litre = 1¾ pints.

Pinzimonio
Neapolitan pizza
Dessert wine and almond biscuits

PINZIMONIO

*The Italian version of French crudités. Go to the market
and find some really fresh vegetables – this is a wonderful
way to enjoy them. Base the varieties and quantities of
vegetables on your own tastes and appetites.*

artichokes, celery, carrots and fennel	*carciofi, carote, sedano, finocchio*
olive oil	*olio d'oliva*
salt and pepper	*sale e pepe*
lemon juice	*limone*

It is vital to select small, young artichokes for this dish. Strip
off their outer leaves and trim the skin off the stalks, leaving
the fleshy centre exposed. Peel the carrots and cut them into
3in sticks. Wash the celery and cut it into sticks of a similar
size. Prepare the fennel in the same way. Arrange the
vegetables on a large dish and put them in the centre of the
table. Give each person an espresso coffee cup or similar small
receptacle. This should contain a good deal of salt, some
pepper, a couple of inches of olive oil and a squeeze of lemon
to dip the vegetables into before eating them.

131

PIZZA NAPOLETANA

Neapolitan pizza

Some bakers sell uncooked bread dough for pizzas. Failing this, dehydrated pizza dough is very easy to use and it tastes surprisingly good. Catarí is the best brand. Avoid frozen pizza bases if you possibly can – most of them really aren't worth eating. If you don't feel like cooking at all you can buy a ready-made pizza to take away from the local pizzeria. The amount of tomatoes and mozzarella you put on top of a homemade pizza is up to you, but don't overdo it or it will overflow in the oven, and don't underdo it as there's nothing worse than a stingy pizza!

one packet of Catarí dehydrated pizza dough per pizza or fresh pizza dough	*una scatola di pizza Catarí*
	impasto per la pizza
olive oil	*olio d'oliva*
fresh or tinned tomatoes	*pomodori freschi/pelati*
anchovies	*acciughe*
a *mozzarella*	*una mozzarella*
capers	*capperi*
black olives without stones	*olive nere snocciolate*
basil or oregano	*basilico/origano*

If you are using uncooked bread dough, you'll need approximately 150g (6oz) of dough per pizza. If you are using Catarí, make up the dough by adding olive oil, and water, in the quantities recommended on the packet. (These will be quite straightforward – look for the words *olio d'oliva* and *acqua* followed by quantities.) Roll it out into a rough circle about ¼in thick and brush with a little olive oil. Chop the tomatoes (if you're using tinned ones drain them well first), and arrange them on top of the pizza dough. Then arrange the anchovies, sliced *mozzarella*, olives, capers and torn basil leaves or oregano on top of the tomatoes. Bake according to the instructions on the packet.

If you are using baker's dough, bake the pizza in a hot oven for about 10 minutes, or until it is brown around the edges and crisp. It should be eaten very hot.

VIN SANTO E CANTUCCI

Dessert wine and almond biscuits

Vin Santo
Cantucci biscuits

Cantucci are hard almond biscuits which are specially made for dipping into Vin Santo.

Vin Santo is made in Tuscany from grapes that have been partially dried before pressing. It's a Tuscan speciality, but can usually be bought elsewhere. It you're staying in an area that makes its own dessert wine, for goodness sake try that! If you're in southern Italy, for example, try Marsala, produced in Sicily, or Malvasia, made all over the South. Or ask for *un vino amabile* or *uno vino abboccato della regione* at your local *enoteca* (wine merchant). If such a thing exists, this should result in the appearance of the local sweet dessert wine.

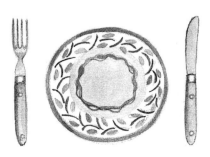

Tomato and *mozzarella* salad
Fish soup
Fresh fruit

INSALATA CAPRESE

Tomato and *mozzarella* salad

2 large tomatoes	*due pomodori grandi*
mozzarella	*mozzarella*
fresh basil	*basilico*
salt and pepper	*sale e pepe*
olive oil	*olio d'oliva*

Slice the tomatoes and the *mozzarella*. Arrange the slices alternately on a plate. Tear the basil leaves into shreds and sprinkle over the salad with some salt, freshly ground black pepper and a little olive oil. Set the dish aside for 20 minutes so that the flavours can combine. *(Serves 4)*

BRODETTO FANESE

Fish soup

Over the centuries every sea port developed its own, traditional recipe for fish soup as a convenient way of using up all the fish that was too small to sell. This recipe comes from Fano in Le Marche. It's a relatively simple one and it won't suffer if you can't get exactly the right varieties of fish. Ask the fishmonger to clean them for you, (me li pulisce per favore?), but be sure to bring the heads home with you for the stock (lasci le teste, perchè mi servono per fare la zuppa di pesce?).

1 stick celery	*sedano*
parsley	*prezzemolo*

1 onion	*una cipolla*
1 carrot	*una carota*
1kg (2lb) of fish made up from a mixture of skate, red mullet, cod, squid, small anglerfish, small dogfish and lobster	*un chilo di pesce misto: razza, triglie, merluzzo, calamaretti, pescatrici, palombetti, aragosta*
6 peppercorns	*grani di pepe*
1 bay leaf	*alloro*
garlic	*aglio*
olive oil	*olio d'oliva*
1 glass of white wine	*vino bianco*
100g (4oz) tinned tomatoes	*pomodori pelati*
bread	*pane*

To make the stock, chop the celery, parsley, half the onion and a carrot. Put them into a pan with the fish heads, the peppercorns, the bay leaf and some water and boil them for half an hour. Then take out the fish heads, strain off the stock and set it aside. Liquidize the remaining ingredients or push them through a sieve before adding them to the stock.

Meanwhile, chop some more parsley, the rest of the onion and two cloves of garlic. Fry gently in a little oil for 2 or 3 minutes. Add the squid, season it with salt and allow it to fry for a moment before pouring in the white wine. Continue to cook until the wine has almost evaporated and then add the tomatoes. Cook for another minute or two before pouring the fish stock into the pan. Turn up the heat and throw in the dogfish, the anglerfish and the lobster. These should be allowed to cook for a 3 or 4 minutes before the cod and mullet go in. Continue to cook the fish over a medium heat for a further 10–15 minutes. When it is ready the fish will start to fall apart.

Toast some bread. Rub it with garlic and lay it in the bottom of a soup tureen. Pour the soup onto the toast in the tureen and serve at once. *(Serves 4)*

Pecorino cheese and broad beans
Baked sardines and artichokes
Stuffed peaches

PECORINO CON LE FAVE

Pecorino cheese and broad beans

This is a typically Tuscan way of either starting or finishing a summer meal.

4kg (9lb) broad beans	*quattro chili di fave*
½kg (1lb) *pecorino*,	*mezzo chilo di pecorino*
fresh or mature	*fresco/staggionato*

Pile 9 or 10 broad bean pods onto a plate for each person and serve with some finely sliced *pecorino*. *Pecorino* is made from ewe's milk. It can be fresh (*fresco*), or mature (*stagionato*). The fresh cheese is quite mild and creamy with a soft, yellow rind. A mature *pecorino* is dark in colour, hard and really quite strong. Choose whichever one you prefer. Cheese shops will often let you taste before you buy (Can I taste it? *Posso assagiarlo?*) You'll find shelling the beans and eating each one with a morsel of cheese a pleasant, time-consuming activity. Your dinner table will have a rustic look about it and you'll find the combination of beans and cheese surprisingly delicious. (*Serves 4*)

SARDE E CARCIOFI

Baked sardines and artichokes

You can either make the breadcrumbs for this dish or buy them ready made from a baker. Ask the fishmonger to clean and fillet the fish for you, (me li pulisce e toglie la spina per favore?)

600g (1lb 5oz) sardines	*seicento grammi di sarde*
4 artichokes	*quattro carciofi*
olive oil	*olio d'oliva*
salt	*sale*
parsley	*prezzemolo*
breadcrumbs	*pangrattato*
lemon juice	*limone*

If you can't buy cleaned and filleted fish you must clean the sardines, remove their heads and then open them out to remove the spines. Rinse under plenty of cold, running water and close them up again so that they look whole.

Take the outer leaves off the artichokes. Cut the prickles off the ends of the remaining leaves and take the skin off the stems. Slice thinly, cutting the artichokes lengthways. Select a fireproof dish of about 25cm (10in) in diameter. Oil it well and arrange a layer of artichoke slices in it. Sprinkle a little salt over the artichokes before putting a layer of fish on top of them. Arrange the fish so that their tails point towards the centre of the dish. Season them with salt, a drizzle of oil and some chopped parsley. Make one more layer each of artichokes and fish, seasoning as before. Sprinkle a handful of breadcrumbs and a drizzle of oil over the dish before putting it into a moderate oven for about 45 minutes, or until the fish and the artichokes are cooked and the breadcrumbs are brown. Pour a little lemon juice over it before serving. *(Serves 4)*

137

PESCHE RIPIENE

Stuffed peaches

This is a very easy dish to make when you grow tired of feasting off fresh peaches. Amaretti are a kind of macaroon.

4 large ripe peaches	*quattro pesche grandi mature*
4 or 5 amaretti	*amaretti*
1 egg yolk	*uova*
2 tablespoons sugar	*zucchero*
knob of butter	*burro*
¼ glass white wine	*vino bianco*

Wash the peaches and cut them in half. Remove the stones and enough of the flesh to make a cavity for the stuffing. Put the flesh in a bowl with the crushed amaretti, egg yolk, butter and sugar. Mix thoroughly and use a teaspoon to put the stuffing into the peaches and smooth it down. Grease an ovenproof dish and arrange the stuffed peaches in it. Pour the wine into the bottom of the dish and bake in a moderate oven for about 25 minutes – the peaches should be tender but firm and the stuffing should still be moist. Serve chilled or at room temperature. *(Serves 4)*

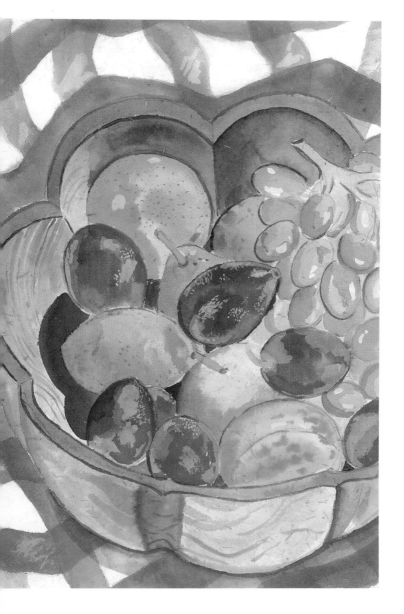

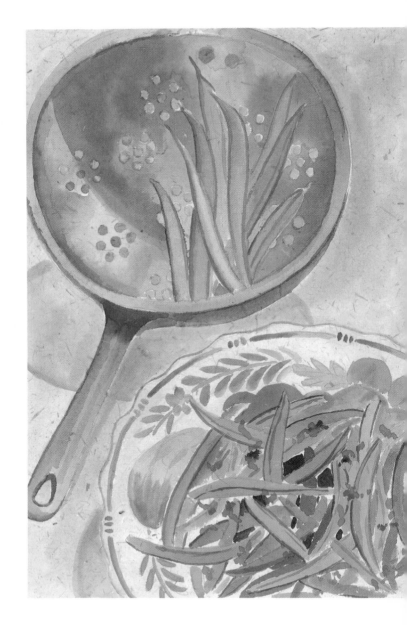

Polenta with meat and tomato sauce
Ice cream

POLENTA

Polenta with meat and tomato sauce

*Polenta, made from maize flour, is one of the staple
ingredients of northern Italian cookery. It often serves as an
alternative to bread, rice or potatoes. In the Veneto it's
sometimes combined with parmesan and a little cream. You
can save time and effort by buying the ready-made frozen or
vacuum packed polenta. To make things even easier, the
number of servings will be written on the packet.*

a pork escalope	*una fettina di maiale*
500g (1lb 8oz) sausage (e.g. Cotechino)	*cinquecento grammi di salsiccia* (e.g. Cotechino)
60g (2oz) butter	*burro*
2 onions	*due cipolle*
1 clove garlic, crushed or chopped	*aglio*
2 tablespoons tomato paste	*concentrato di pomodoro*
salt and pepper	*sale e pepe*
2 cups water	*acqua*
polenta, ready-made frozen	*polenta surgelata*

Cut the pork and the sausage into small pieces. Heat the
butter in a pan and fry the peeled and chopped onions until
transparent. Add the meat and continue frying until golden
brown. Add the crushed or finely chopped garlic. Continue to
fry gently for a minute before putting in the tomato paste,
seasoning and water. Stir to combine and then bring to the
boil. Reduce the heat and simmer for 1½ hours, or until the
meat is very tender and the sauce is a good, thick consistency.

141

You may find that you have to add a little water during the cooking time.

Turn the defrosted *polenta* into a fireproof dish, make a deep trough in the top with a wooden spoon and pour the sauce into it. Put into a hot oven for about 10 minutes to heat through. Serve at once with a full-bodied red wine. *(Serves 4)*

GELATO

Ice cream

Find out where the best local ice cream comes from – go somewhere that makes it on the premises if you can: Dove posso comprare del gelato fresco? (Where can I buy some fresh ice cream?)

Veal escalopes and ham cooked in white wine
Spinach
Peaches in white wine

SALTIMBOCCA ALLA ROMANA

Veal escalopes and ham cooked in white wine

*After pasta and pizza, this is probably the most famous
Italian dish. Veal infused with the flavours of sage and ham
is truly delicious.*

12 thin slices of veal	*dodici fettine di vitello*
300g (10oz) Parma ham	*trecento grammi di prosciutto crudo*
fresh sage leaves	*salvia*
cocktail sticks	*stecchini*
salt and pepper	*sale e pepe*
50g (1¾oz) butter	*burro*
½ glass white wine	*vino bianco*

Lay the veal out on the chopping board and flatten it out by
beating with a meat mallet, a rolling pin or, failing all else, a
bottle. Divide the slices of ham into 12 equal pieces. Place
half a sage leaf – any more would be too much – and a slice of
ham on top of each piece of veal, securing them with a
cocktail stick. Season with salt and pepper. Heat the butter in
a large frying pan and sauté the *saltimbocca*. Do not cook it for
too long on the ham side or the ham will dry out and become
hard. The entire process should take about 12 minutes in all.
Arrange the meat on a serving dish with the ham slices facing
upwards. Remove the cocktail sticks and put the *saltimbocca*
in the oven to keep warm. Pour the wine into the frying pan
and boil rapidly, stirring to mix the wine and juices into a
sauce. Add a small knob of butter and as soon as it melts pour
the sauce over the meat and serve at once. *(Serves 4)*

SPINACI TRASCINATI

Spinach

Spinach that has simply been boiled is not considered to be adequately cooked in Italy. This treatment greatly increases the flavour and is said to make it more digestible.

1kg (2lb) spinach	*un chilo di spinaci*
3 cloves garlic, chopped	*aglio*
olive oil	*olio d'oliva*
salt and pepper	*sale e pepe*

Scald the spinach in boiling water, leaving the lid off the saucepan so that it doesn't lose colour. Drain the spinach and, when it's cool enough, squeeze as much water out of it as you can. Use the palms of your hands – or the side of a colander if this goes against the grain. Heat some oil in a frying pan and fry the chopped garlic in it. Add the spinach as soon as the garlic begins to brown. Season with salt and pepper and fry gently until the spinach has absorbed the flavour of the garlic – 2 or 3 minutes at the most. Serve hot.

Alternatively, the drained spinach can be cooked in melted butter over a low flame for about 10 minutes. *(Serves 4)*

PESCHE IN VINO BIANCO

Peaches in white wine

peaches	*pesche*
dry white wine	*vino bianco secco*

Peel and slice the peaches. Arrange the slices in a bowl and pour enough dry, white wine over them to cover. Allow the flavours to combine by leaving them in the fridge for at least 2 hours before serving.

Neapolitan *croûtons*
Chicken breasts cooked in Marsala
French bean salad
Fruit salad

CROSTINI ALLA NAPOLITANA

Neapolitan *croûtons*

The quantities for this recipe will depend on the number of croûtons you decide to make – one mozzarella will certainly be enough for four of you.

bread	*pane*
olive oil	*olio d'oliva*
a mozzarella cheese	*una mozzarella*
anchovies	*acciughe*
1 tomato	*un pomodoro*
pepper	*pepe*
oregano	*origano*

Cut some rather stale bread into 1cm (½in) slices and remove the crusts. If necessary, cut the slices in half to make pieces of about the size of a playing card. Heat some olive oil in a frying pan and fry them on one side only. Oil an oven-proof dish large enough to hold all the slices of bread. Put them in with the uncooked side downwards. On the cooked side arrange a slice of *mozzarella*, an anchovy and a slice of tomato. Season each *crostino* with pepper and a pinch of oregano. Drizzle a little oil over the dish and put it into a medium oven for about 10 minutes, or until the cheese has melted and the underside of the bread is cooked. Eat very hot. *(Serves 4)*

PETTO DI POLLO

Chicken breasts cooked in Marsala

Chicken breasts are sold ready-boned. Poultry is generally sold by the poulterer (pollaiolo) rather than the butcher.

4 boned chicken breasts	*quattro petti di pollo*
white flour	*farina*
salt and pepper	*sale e pepe*
a knob of butter	*burro*
olive oil	*olio d'oliva*
a glass of Marsala dessert wine	*Marsala all'uovo*

Trim the meat and use a rolling pin to flatten it out as much as possible. Dust with flour and season with salt and pepper.

Heat the butter with a little oil in a thick frying pan and brown the chicken quickly on one side. Turn the meat and pour a glass of Marsala over it. Cover and continue to cook very slowly for a further 15 minutes. *(Serves 4)*

INSALATA DI FAGIOLINI

French bean salad

½kg (1lb) French beans	*mezzo chilo di fagiolini*
2 anchovies	*acciughe*
garlic	*aglio*
parsley	*prezzemolo*
marjoram	*maggiorana*
mint	*menta*
2 tablespoons olive oil	*olio d'oliva*
1 teaspoon vinegar	*aceto*

Cook the beans in boiling, salted water and then arrange them on a serving dish. While they are cooking chop the anchovies and garlic together with the mint, parsley and marjoram. Put the herbs, garlic and anchovies in a cup and add the oil and vinegar, adjusting the proportions to taste. Mix the sauce well and pour it over the beans while they are still hot. Chill before serving. *(Serves 4)*

MACEDONIA

Fruit salad

Another way of enjoying the abundance of Mediterranean fruits. Ideally, you should make the salad before you go out in the morning and leave it in the fridge. By suppertime it will be ice cold and the lemon juice and sugar will have combined with the fruit juices to form a glorious syrup.

peaches	*pesche*
apricots	*albicocche*
figs	*fichi*
seedless grapes	*acini d'uva senza semi*
lemon juice	*limone*
sugar	*zucchero*

Peel the fruit, cut it up into small squares and put it in a bowl. Sprinkle a little sugar and lemon juice over it and leave it to chill for a minimum of 6 hours.

147

Asparagus *risotto*
Strawberries in red wine

RISOTTO CON ASPARAGI

Asparagus *risotto*

Risotto was originally a northern Italian dish. This recipe, however, comes from Le Marche. Before starting to cook clear your mind of the mystique that surrounds risotto making at home. Arborio rice is the secret of success and in Italy it's readily available in even the smallest of grocers. Use a stock cube (Dadi Knorr di pollo) if you don't have any fresh chicken stock.

½kg (1lb) asparagus	*mezzo chilo di asparagi*
1 onion	*una cipolla*
50g (1½oz) cooked ham	*cinquanta grammi di prosciutto cotto*
butter	*burro*
olive oil	*olio d'oliva*
400g (14oz) *arborio* rice	*riso arborio*
½ glass dry white wine	*vino bianco secco*
approx 1½ litres (2½ pints) chicken stock	
salt and pepper	*sale e pepe*
parmesan	*parmigiano*

Cook the asparagus in boiling salted water. Tie it in bundles and stand these in a tall saucepan with a couple of inches of water in the bottom. Cover it and steam until tender. How long this takes will depend upon the size of the asparagus. Expect to wait for anything from 5 to 20 minutes.

Chop the onion and the cooked ham finely. Heat a knob of butter and a little olive oil in a thick frying pan. Fry until the onion is translucent and then add the rice. Stir well to combine the ingredients and pour in the wine. Wait until the wine has almost evaporated before adding the first ladleful of stock, stirring all the time. As the stock is absorbed, continue to add more, never putting in more than a ladleful at a time.

When the rice is about half cooked cut the tips from the asparagus and set them aside. Mash or blend the remaining stems and then mix this purée with the rice. Season with salt and pepper. Before taking the pan off the heat add to the *risotto* the asparagus tips, a knob of butter and a good handful of parmesan. Stir carefully to blend the ingredients without destroying the asparagus tips. Allow the *risotto* to rest for a few minutes before serving.

Risotto can be made in a matter of minutes with a pressure cooker. Asparagus wouldn't be ideal for this treatment, but you could replace it with chopped, frozen spinach, finely chopped courgettes or any frozen vegetable. Follow the same procedure, adding 1 litre (1¾ pints) of water to each ½kg (1lb) of rice. Allow the *risotto* to cook for 5 minutes after the pan has come up to pressure. *(Serves 4)*

FRAGOLE

Strawberries in red wine

Strawberries start to arrive in the shops in the early spring. It is rather more common to eat them with wine in Italy than with cream. Some people prefer to use lemon juice as it complements the sweetness of the strawberries without masking their flavour.

strawberries	*fragole*
red wine	*vino rosso*
sugar	*zucchero*

Hull and rinse the strawberries. Dry them gently on kitchen

paper or a clean cloth. Cut them in half and put them into a bowl. Pour one glass of wine over them for every ½kg (1lb) of fruit. Sprinkle with sugar and put in the fridge for an hour or two before serving.

Stewed peppers and tomatoes
Baked Sardinian omelette with courgettes
Fresh fruit (Muscat grapes – *uva moscata*)

PEPERONATA

Stewed peppers and tomatoes

This recipe can be served as a starter or as an addition to the main course. It's equally good hot or cold.

5 red peppers	*cinque peperoni rossi*
1 large onion	*una cipolla grande*
½kg (1lb) tomatoes	*mezzo chilo di pomodori*
2 cloves garlic	*aglio*
olive oil	*olio d'oliva*
oregano	*origano*
1 bay leaf	*alloro*
salt	*sale*

Wash the peppers and cut them into wide strips. Remove the seeds. Chop the onion. Peel the tomatoes by dipping them into boiling water and stripping off the skin. Cut them into quarters. Peel and chop a couple of cloves of garlic. Brown the chopped onion in a little oil with the garlic, oregano and the bay leaf. Add the peppers and the seasoning and cook quite rapidly for about 10 minutes. Now add the tomatoes and continue to simmer for about 30 minutes or until the mixture thickens – leave the lid off the pan. *(Serves 4)*

FRITTATA DI ZUCCHINI

Baked omelette with courgettes

*The grated courgettes in this recipe give the omelette a
delightful texture.*

3 courgettes	*tre zucchini*
fresh breadcrumbs	*(pane)*
milk	*latte*
sugar	*zucchero*
salt	*sale*
parmesan	*parmigiano*
lemon rind	*un limone*
6 eggs	*sei uova*
olive oil	*olio d'oliva*

Grate the courgettes coarsely and then squeeze the water out
of them between your palms. Soak a handful of breadcrumbs
in a little milk. Stir a pinch of sugar, a pinch of salt, a handful
of parmesan and some grated lemon rind into the milk and
breadcrumbs. Beat the eggs and add them to the other
ingredients, stirring well once more. Grease the inside of a
fireproof dish with oil or butter and sprinkle breadcrumbs
over it. Pour in the egg mixture and cook in a medium oven
for about 25 minutes or until fairly firm and golden brown.
(Serves 4)

> Spaghetti with basil sauce
> Baked cod with mushrooms
> Fresh fruit

SPAGHETTI AL PESTO GENOVESE

Spaghetti with basil sauce

Pesto sauce is a Genoese speciality. It's a strongly flavoured sauce, made with fresh basil, olive oil, pine kernels, parmesan and seasoning. Traditionally, pesto is made by crushing the ingredients in a pestle and mortar. You needn't go to this extreme, however. Ready made pesto is generally very good and you can usually buy jars of it in supermarkets or larger grocers (use sparingly).

½kg (1lb) spaghetti	*mezzo chilo di spaghetti*
pesto sauce	*pesto*

Cook the spaghetti in plenty of salted water. Drain, and turn it into a bowl. Add a teaspoon or two of pesto sauce, to taste, and mix it in well. Adjust seasoning if necessary. *(Serves 4)*

MERLUZZI AL PIATTO

Baked cod with mushrooms

Ask the fishmonger to clean the cod for you, (li può pulire per favore?). You can either make your own breadcrumbs or buy them ready made from a baker.

2 cod weighing approx ½kg (1lb) each	*due merluzzi di mezzo chilo circa ciascuno*
butter	*burro*
¼ onion	*una cipolla*

200g (7oz) cultivated mushrooms	*due cento grammi di funghi coltivati*
salt	*sale*
breadcrumbs	*pangrattato*
1 teaspoon grated parmesan	*parmigiano*
¼ glass dry white wine	*vino bianco secco*
lemon juice	*limone*
parsley	*prezzemolo*

Open the fish out. Flatten them and then rinse under plenty of running water and pat dry. Butter an oval fireproof dish big enough to hold both fish. Arrange a layer of chopped onion and finely sliced mushrooms on the bottom of the dish. Put the fish on top of the vegetables with their backs facing upwards. Season with a little salt and then cover with breadcrumbs, parmesan and melted butter. Pour in enough wine to just cover the bottom of the dish. Put into a hot oven for 12–15 minutes, or until the fish are cooked and the cheese and breadcrumbs have just begun to go brown. Before serving, pour a little lemon juice over the dish and garnish with chopped parsley. *(Serves 4)*

INSALATA DI FINOCCHIO

Fennel salad

3 fennel bulbs	*tre finocchi*
6 tablespoons olive oil	*olio d'oliva*
2 tablespoons vinegar	*aceto*
1 tablespoon chopped parsley	*prezzemolo*
salt and pepper	*sale e pepe*

Cut the fennel into thin slices and put it into a salad bowl. Combine the oil with the other ingredients. Stir until the salt dissolves and then pour over the fennel. *(Serves 4)*

Pasta salad with courgettes
Pork escalopes with tomato and caper sauce
Jewish fennel
Fresh fruit

A meal for hearty appetites!

PASTA CON ZUCCHINI

Pasta salad with courgettes

The combination of hot courgettes with cold pasta is surprisingly pleasant. Do be sure to add a drop of vinegar to the oil and basil in the salad bowl – it takes away the taste of frying.

1 clove of garlic	*aglio*
1 small onion	*una cipolla piccola*
½kg (1lb) courgettes	*mezzo chilo di zucchini*
olive oil	*olio d'oliva*
salt	*sale*
½kg (1lb) short pasta such as *penne, conchiglie* or *rigatoni*	*mezzo chilo di pasta tipo penne, conchiglie o rigatoni*
fresh basil	*basilico*
fresh parsley, chopped	*prezzemolo*
pepper	*pepe*
vinegar	*aceto*

Peel and chop the garlic cloves and onion as finely as you can. Cut the courgettes into slices. Heat the olive oil in a frying pan. Fry the courgettes until lightly browned. Drain them on kitchen paper (Scottex) or brown paper and sprinkle them with salt. Fry the chopped onion and garlic. Cook the pasta in the usual way and then rinse it with plenty of cold water. Put fresh oil, roughly torn basil leaves, chopped parsley, pepper and a drop of vinegar into a bowl. Add the pasta, onion, garlic and courgettes. Combine the ingredients and serve immediately. Cold pasta salads can be made out of numerous different combinations of ingredients – try Mozzarella, tomatoes and chopped basil. *(Serves 4)*

SCALLOPINA DI MANZO ALLA PIZZAIOLA

Pork escalopes with tomato and caper sauce

Meat cooked in a pizzaiola sauce is a traditional dish in Naples and the Campania. Almost any meat except lamb can be used.

1 kg (2lb) fresh tomatoes	*due chili pomodori*
olive oil	*olio d'oliva*
a spoonful of capers	*capperi*
3 large cloves garlic	*aglio*
salt and pepper	*sale e pepe*
basil	*basilico*
4 escalopes (pork, veal, beef)	*quattro fettine (di maiale, vitello, bistecca)*
butter	*burro*

Dip the tomatoes into boiling water and peel them. Make a *pizzaiola* sauce by frying the peeled and chopped tomatoes with a little olive oil, garlic, capers, salt and pepper. Add roughly torn fresh basil leaves just before the sauce is cooked. Don't overcook it – the tomatoes should retain their colour and some of their texture.

Trim the meat, beat it in order to flatten it out as much as possible and season well with salt and pepper. Heat the butter in a wide frying pan and fry the escalopes in a single layer until they are lightly browned on each side. Spread the sauce thickly over each escalope, cover the pan and continue cooking for a further 5 minutes. *(Serves 4)*

155

FINOCCHI ALLA GIUDEA

Jewish fennel

4 fennel bulbs	*quattro finocchi*
parsley	*prezzemolo*
4 cloves garlic	*aglio*
olive oil	*olio d'oliva*
salt and pepper	*sale e pepe*

Wash the fennel, discarding any damaged outer leaves. Cut the bulbs in half and leave them to stand in cold water for a few minutes. Now rinse them under running water, opening the leaves out slightly to dislodge any earth that may be trapped between them. Chop the parsley and garlic together as finely as you can. Arrange the fennel in a fireproof dish and sprinkle the garlic and parsley mixture over them. Drizzle with oil, add a little water, a pinch of salt and some pepper. Cover the dish and cook gently for 15 minutes. Then remove the lid and cook rapidly until the fennel is tender. *(Serves 4)*

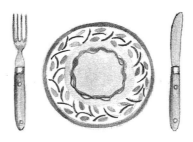

Fried *boletus* mushrooms
Red chicory salad
Ricotta flavoured with coffee

PORCINI FRITTI

Fried *boletus* mushrooms

Porcini mushrooms have an exquisite flavour that is hard to describe. They are much richer than our own field mushrooms and served with croûtons and a salad they will be more than adequate as a main course. Choose mushrooms of medium size – the very large ones have a tendency to crumble and the smaller ones can be a little bit tough – 2 or 3 per person will be ample.

fresh *boletus* mushrooms	*porcini freschi*
flour	*farina*
olive oil	*olio d'oliva*
3 cloves garlic	*aglio*
salt and pepper	*sale e pepe*
1 tablespoon chopped parsley	*prezzemolo*
lemon juice	*limone*
croûtons	*crostini di pane*

Clean the mushrooms thoroughly by rinsing until the water is clear. Don't leave them to soak as they will lose their flavour. Scrape the earth off the stems and wash them as well.

Prepare *croûtons* by frying or toasting the bread (*pane*).

Cut the mushrooms into moderate-sized slices and coat each slice in flour. Heat some oil in a frying pan and put 3 whole cloves of garlic into it. Allow the garlic to brown slightly before lifting it out. Now put the mushrooms into the pan, season with salt and pepper and fry briskly for a few minutes. Add a spoonful of chopped parsley before taking the pan off the heat. Squeeze some lemon juice over the mushrooms and serve them with hot *croûtons*. *(Serves 4)*

INSALATA DI RADICCHIO ROSSO

Red chicory salad

Use red chicory and dress with oil and vinegar in the usual way.

RICOTTA AL CAFFE

Ricotta flavoured with coffee

Ricotta – a soft, white cheese made from ewe's milk – is a very useful base for simple puddings. Make sure that it's really fresh when you buy it and don't store it uncovered in the fridge as it tends to absorb other flavours. There are many sorts of Marsala – you could use Marsala al Caffè.

300g (10oz) Ricotta	*tre etti di ricotta*
2 tablespoons finely ground coffee	*caffè macinato*
2 tablespoons sugar	*zucchero*
1 tablespoon Marsala dessert wine	*Marsala*

Beat the sugar, Marsala and coffee into the *ricotta*. Stir together until smooth and chill for at least 2 hours before serving. *(Serves 4)*

Stuffed tomatoes
Green salad
Pears with *pecorino* cheese

Quick to prepare after a day out.

POMODORI RIPIENI

Stuffed tomatoes

Buy stuffed tomatoes from the *rosticceria* or *tavola calda*. Two each should be enough. They are usually stuffed with a mixture of mince and rice.

INSALATA VERDE

Green salad

As this is the cook's night off I suggest that you opt for a very simple salad. The Italians often add flavour to their salads by using wild greens such as purslane, dandelion or arugula. Each area tends to have its own selection of wild salad greens and its own dialect names for them. If you want to try them, look out for likely looking bundles at the greengrocer's. Failing that, ask for *insalata di campo* (field salad), and see what you get! Don't use too many wild greens in proportion to lettuce (*lattuga*), as they can be very bitter. Salads are generally dressed with virgin olive oil (*olio d'oliva vergine*), a good wine vinegar (*aceto*) and a sprinkling of salt (*sale*). It's quite common to bring the oil and vinegar to the table so that everyone can dress their own serving of salad. Some people prefer to substitute lemon juice for the vinegar.

159

PERE CON PECORINO

Pears with *pecorino* cheese

Pears and *pecorino* (sheep's cheese) marry with the same success as cheddar and apples. The combination was first discovered in Abruzzo in the south of Italy where it still has a place among the traditional dishes of the region. Be sure to select pears that are ripe but not soft.

Beef California
Green salad
Cherries in red wine

MANZO ALLA CALIFORNIANA

Beef California

*Who knows why the Lombard cook who invented this recipe
gave it such an outlandish name! Don't be put off by the
long cooking time – you won't need to do anything after the
first 15 minutes.*

½ onion	*una cipolla*
1 carrot	*una carota*
50g (1½oz) butter	*burro*
700g (1lb 8oz) rump steak	*settecento grammi di bistecca di filetto*
seasoned flour	*farina*
1 tablespoon strong red wine vinegar	*aceto forte*
200ml (7fl oz) water	*acqua*
200ml (7fl oz) cream	*panna da cucina*
2 cups rice	*riso*

Chop half an onion into four sections and dice the carrot. Fry
the vegetables in the butter until the onion is transparent.
Dust the meat with seasoned flour and put it in the pan with
the vegetables. Fry gently on both sides to seal. When it's
well browned pour the vinegar over it and turn up the heat.
Allow the vinegar to evaporate before pouring in the water
and then the cream. Cover the pan and simmer for 3 hours, or
until the meat is tender. You may need to add a little more
water during the cooking time. When it's tender, cut the meat
into thick slices. Sieve the gravy, adding more cream if it's a
bit sparse. Serve with boiled rice. *(Serves 4)*

INSALATA VERDE

Green salad

(See page 159)

CILIEGE AL VINO ROSSO

Cherries in red wine

Use any full-bodied red wine for this recipe. Try to get large cherries – morello cherries are ideal.

1½ glasses red wine	*vino rosso*
100g (4oz) of sugar	*zucchero*
1 tablespoon black cherry jam	*marmellata di amarene*
pinch cinnamon	*cannella*
grated rind of 1 lemon	*un limone*
½kg (1lb) dark cherries	*mezzo chilo di ciliege*

Put the wine, sugar, jam, cinnamon and grated lemon rind into a saucepan. Heat gently until the sugar dissolves. Meanwhile, wash the cherries and remove their stalks. It isn't really necessary to stone them. When the sugar has dissolved add the fruit to the wine mixture in the pan. Bring to the boil, reduce the heat and simmer, covered, for about 20 minutes. Put the cherries and the syrup into a dish and chill before serving. *(Serves 4)*

Spaghetti with tomatoes, capers and olives
Green salad
Cream cheese pudding

SPAGHETTI ALLA PUTTANESCA

Spaghetti with tomatoes, capers and olives

This recipe originated in the Lazio. Take care with the chilli pepper – if you really enjoy hot food try cooking the seeds as well.

2 cloves of garlic	*aglio*
olive oil	*olio d'oliva*
½ a fresh chilli, de-seeded	*peperoncino*
8 anchovies	*acciughe*
1 tin tomatoes	*pomodori pelati*
100g (4oz) stoned black olives	*un etto di olive nere snocciolate*
1 tablespoon capers	*capperi*
1 tablespoon chopped parsley	*prezzemolo*
400g (14oz) spaghetti	*spaghetti*

Chop the garlic and fry it gently in oil with the chilli and the anchovies. Stir in the other ingredients and continue to simmer while the pasta cooks. Drain the pasta and toss it in the hot sauce. Serve immediately. *(Serves 4)*

INSALATA VERDE

Green salad

(See page 159)

MASCARPONE

Cream cheese pudding

*Mascarpone is a double cream cheese made in Lombardy.
Rather like ricotta, it serves as a good basis for desserts.
This one looks particularly attractive when served in
individual glasses or dishes.*

2 eggs	*uova*
300g (10oz) *mascarpone*	*trecento grammi di mascarpone*
50g (2oz) sugar	*zucchero*
2 tablespoons brandy	*cognac*

Separate the eggs. Add the yolks to the cheese and sugar. Beat
until the mixture is light and fluffy. Beat in the brandy.
Whisk the egg whites until they are really firm and then fold
them into the cheese mixture. Chill well before serving.
(Serves 4)

Roast chicken
Glazed fruit tart

POLLO ARROSTO

Roast chicken

Buy a roast chicken and roast potatoes (*patate arrosto*) from the *rosticceria* or *tavola calda*. Serve with a green salad (page 159).

CROSTATA DI FRUTTA

Glazed fruit tart

Buy a fruit tart from the *pasticceria*.

Cold meat *antipasto*
Piedmontese fondue
Watermelon

ANTIPASTO MISTO

Cold meat *antipasto*

Buy a selection of cold ham and salami, opting – as usual – for the local specialities. If you are staying in Emilia Romagna, you will find a wide variety of locally produced salami and hams. If in doubt, ask: *c'é un salame/un prosciutto della zona?*

Allow approximately 50g (2oz) of meat per person. Arrange the meat on a platter with some black olives and a selection of *giardiniera* (vegetables preserved in oil or vinegar). They can be bought in jars from a grocer or supermarket, or loose from a good *rosticceria*.

FONDUTA PIEDMONTESE

Piedmontese fondue

This is one of the most famous northern Italian dishes. Fontina is a Piedmontese cheese but you will have no difficulty in buying it elsewhere. This fondue is exquisite with truffles. Piedmont produces the best white truffles in the country. The season runs from October to March. Without them it is still very good indeed, so don't be put off if you can't get them. Ideally you should use a double saucepan to melt the cheese. If you don't have one use a bowl in a pan of water instead.

450g (1lb) *fontina*	*quattrocentocinquanta grammi di fontina*
200ml (7fl oz) milk	*latte fresco*
4 egg yolks	*uova*
knob of butter	*burro*
salt and pepper	*sale e pepe*
a few slices of white truffle	*tartufi bianchi*
bread sticks or toast	*grissini*

Dice the cheese and cover it with the milk. Leave it to soak for about 2 hours. Put the cheese and milk with the beaten egg yolks and butter in the top of a saucepan. Cook over a moderate heat, stirring continually. As soon as the cheese has melted and amalgamated with the eggs, season with salt and pepper and pour into small bowls. A few paper-thin slices of white truffle should be floated on the surface of each bowl.

Serve with a full-bodied red wine and thin slices of hot toast or *grissini* to dip into the fondue. *(Serves 4)*

COCOMERO or ANGURIA

Watermelon

Buy a watermelon – either whole or in slices. It tastes much better if it's chilled so try to buy it in the morning and keep it in the fridge until suppertime.

Tuscan bread salad
Egyptian omelette
Mixed salad
Whipped Marsala custard

PANZANELLA

Tuscan bread salad

Do give this recipe a try. It may not look very exciting on paper but you will find that it makes a delicious and unusual summer salad. Tuscan bread goes stale very quickly and there's something satisfying about finding a use for it. Make sure you use one of the sweet, red onions. I haven't given exact quantities, it's not that kind of recipe. Add enough olive oil to flavour the bread without turning it soggy.

stale white bread	*pane bianco raffermo*
½kg (1lb) ripe tomatoes	*mezzo chilo di pomodori maturi*
fresh basil leaves	*basilico*
a small tin of tuna in oil	*tonno sott'olio*
5 chopped anchovies	*acciughe*
1 red onion	*una cipolla rossa*
2 tablespoons capers	*capperi*
olive oil	*olio d'oliva*
salt and pepper	*sale e pepe*
garlic	*aglio*

167

Immerse the bread in cold water and soak for 30 minutes. While it's soaking chop the tomatoes and the anchovies and put them into a large bowl with the roughly torn basil leaves and the tuna. When the bread is completely saturated squeeze the water out of it between your palms and crumble it into the bowl with the other ingredients. Mix the oil with salt, pepper and a little finely chopped garlic in a small bowl. Chill and pour the dressing over the salad just before serving. *(Serves 4)*

FRITTATA ALL'EGIZIANA

Egyptian omelette

You can serve frittata hot or cold – when it's cold it makes a good filling for a crusty roll. Most cooked vegetables or meats are suitable as ingredients. If you use cooked spinach follow the instructions for spinaci trascinati (page 144) before adding it to the eggs. Basil, tomatoes and chopped ham make another delicious filling and so does finely chopped left-over spaghetti with tomato sauce.

1 aubergine	*una melanzana*
1 large courgette	*uno zucchino*
olive oil	*olio d'oliva*
parsley	*prezzemolo*
6 eggs	*sei uova*
salt and pepper	*sale e pepe*
2 tablespoons of grated parmesan	*parmigiano grattugiato*
a pinch of salt	*sale*

Cut the aubergine into small cubes and the courgette into slightly larger ones without skinning either of them. Heat a little oil in a pan and cook the vegetables with a pinch of salt and a little chopped parsley. Beat the eggs together and add the seasoning and the grated parmesan. As soon as the vegetables are cooked turn the eggs into the pan. Flatten the *frittata* with a palette knife and shake the pan to prevent it from sticking. Cook over a medium heat for about 5 minutes, or until the underside is nicely browned. Slide it onto a plate and then slip it back into the pan to cook the other side. *(Serves 4)*

INSALATA MISTA

Mixed salad

Make up a mixed salad with lettuce (*lattuga*), tomatoes (*pomodori*), grated carrots (*carote grattugiate*) and torn basil leaves (*basilico*). Dress with virgin olive oil (*olio d'oliva vergine*), lemon juice and salt.

ZABAGLIONE

Whipped Marsala custard

Zabaglione is a marvellously rich egg custard flavoured with Marsala and lemon rind. Traditionally doctors prescribed it for patients who needed building up!

4 egg yolks	*uova*
4 tablespoons of sugar	*zucchero*
8 tablespoons of Marsala dessert wine	*Marsala*
grated peel from one lemon	*un limone*
vanilla essence (optional)	*essenza di vaniglia*

Place the egg yolks and sugar in a bowl. Put the bowl into a pan of hot water. (Use a double saucepan if you have one.) Heat slowly, beating continuously with a wire whisk if you have one, or fork. After approximately 5 minutes the sugar will dissolve and the eggs will turn pale yellow and become creamy and smooth. Continue beating while you add the

Marsala a drop at a time. Stir in the lemon rind, and the vanilla essence if you are using it. Continue to cook over a gentle heat and to beat the mixture continuously. After 15 minutes or so the *zabaglione* will thicken and double in size. Pour into individual glasses or dishes and cool completely before serving with *amaretti* biscuits. *(Serves 4)*

Ricotta and spinach *ravioli* with butter and sage
Artichoke salad and Parma ham
Fresh fruit

RAVIOLI DI RICOTTA E SPINACI CON BURRO E SALVIA

Ricotta and spinach *ravioli* with butter and sage

Frozen ravioli comes in packs of 250g (9oz) or 500g (18oz). Allow 150g (5oz) per person. Fresh ravioli can be bought at a baker's or grocer's.

600g (1lb 5oz) spinach and Ricotta *ravioli* fresh or frozen	*seicento grammi di ravioli di ricotta e spinaci freschi/ surgelati*
butter	*burro*
fresh sage leaves	*salvia*
parmesan	*parmigiano*

Cook 12 *ravioli* at a time in plenty of boiling, salted water. They usually take about 7 minutes to cook, but start testing them as soon as they rise to the surface of the pan. Remove the cooked *ravioli* with a slotted spoon, spread them out on a plate and keep them warm – don't pile them up because they'll stick together.

Melt a good knob of butter in a pan and remove the sage leaves from their stems. When the butter is really hot put the

170

sage into it and fry rapidly. The leaves will become crisp just before they burn – this is what you should aim for. Tip the cooked ravioli into the pan with the butter and sage. Add plenty of grated parmesan and black pepper, stir gently over the heat and serve at once. *(Serves 4)*

INSALATA DI CARCIOFI CON PROSCIUTTO CRUDO

Artichoke salad and Parma ham

Parma ham tends to dry up in the fridge so don't buy it too far in advance.

4 artichokes	*quattro carciofi*
1 lemon	*un limone*
olive oil	*olio d'oliva*
salt	*sale*
200g (7oz) Parma ham	*duecento grammi di prosciutto crudo*

Remove all the hard outside leaves from the artichokes. Cut the stalks off quite close to the head. Peel the hard skin off the remaining sections of stalk. Cut off the top half of the artichokes and throw them away. Cut the remaining part in half to expose the bristly 'choke' and remove that with a knife. Squeeze lemon juice all over them to prevent discolouration and then cut them lengthwise into paper-thin strips. Season with more lemon juice, oil and salt. Serve with slices of Parma ham. *(Serves 4)*

Asparagus bundles
Grilled red mullet
Chicory salad
A ready-made chilled dessert

FAGOTTINI DI ASPARAGI

Asparagus bundles

This isn't a recipe in which exact quantities can be given as everything depends on the size of the asparagus. You should aim to make one good bundle for each person – three sturdy pieces of asparagus should do it. You'll need a slice of Parma ham for each bundle.

asparagus	*asparagi*
Parma ham	*prosciutto crudo*
salt and pepper	*sale e pepe*
parmesan	*parmigiano*
butter	*burro*

Clean the asparagus and then cook it in bundles in boiling, salted water. Drain it as soon as it's tender and make up the bundles by wrapping three pieces of asparagus in a slice of ham. Grease a fireproof dish and arrange the bundles in it. Season with salt and pepper. Sprinkle with grated parmesan and put a few dabs of butter on top of the cheese. Cook in a moderate oven for about 20 minutes. Serve immediately. (*Serves 4*)

TRIGLIE ALLA VENEZIANA

Grilled red mullet

*This traditional Venetian dish is equally good hot or cold. If
your kitchen doesn't have a grill don't despair – you can
coat the fish in flour and fry them just as well. Ask the
fishmonger to clean the fish for you, (Me le pulisce per
favore?).*

4 red mullet	*quattro triglie*
mint	*menta*
4 small garlic cloves	*aglio*
olive oil	*olio d'oliva*
1 small onion	*una cipolla*
1 glass white wine	*vino bianco*
1 tablespoon white wine vinegar	*aceto*
1 lemon	*un limone*
parsley	*prezzemolo*

Rinse the fish under running water and pat them dry. Put a
few mint leaves and a clove of garlic inside each one. Prepare
for grilling by scoring diagonally twice on each side and
brushing with oil. Cook under a medium heat for about 8
minutes each side – although this will depend on the size of
the fish.

While the fish are cooking make the sauce. Chop a little
onion very finely and fry in oil until it's translucent but not
brown. Pour the wine and the vinegar into the pan and
simmer until reduced by half – this may take as long as 15
minutes. Arrange the fish in a serving dish and when the
sauce has cooled pour it over them. Decorate with lemon
slices and chopped parsley. *(Serves 4)*

175

PUNTARELLE

White chicory salad

1 head of white chicory	*cicoria belga*
2 or 3 garlic cloves	*aglio*
olive oil	*olio d'oliva*
vinegar	*aceto*
salt and pepper	*sale e pepe*

Wash and dry the chicory carefully and put it into a bowl. Chop two or three garlic cloves and combine them with about three tablespoons of oil and one of vinegar. Season with salt and pepper. Put the salad into a large bowl and add the dressing. Leave it to stand for about half an hour before serving. *(Serves 4)*

UN DOLCE SEMI-FREDDO

A ready-made chilled dessert

Select a ready-made dessert from the cold cabinet of your local grocer or large bar.

Potato tart
Peppers in the pan
Fresh fruit – figs (*fichi*)

TORTA DI PATATE

Potato tart

This dish is just as delicious sliced and served cold as an antipasto.

2 large potatoes	*patate*
1 egg	*uova*
1 teaspoon salt	*sale*
pepper	*pepe*
pinch of nutmeg	*noce moscata*
2 tablespoons flour	*farina*
2 tablespoons milk	*latte*
¼ cup grated parmesan	*parmigiano*
2 tablespoons olive oil	*olio d'oliva*

Peel and grate the raw potatoes. Put them in a bowl and mix with the beaten egg, seasoning and nutmeg. Add the flour and milk alternately, putting in a little at a time and stirring carefully to avoid lumps. Add the parmesan and stir again to combine. The mixture shouldn't be too solid – you can always add a little more milk if it is.

Oil a pie dish and spread the potato mixture out to a thickness of about an inch. Sprinkle a little more parmesan on top and bake for about 40 minutes in a hot oven. There should be a golden crust on the top and the bottom. *(Serves 4)*

PEPERONI IN PADELLA

Peppers in the pan

4 red peppers	*quattro peperoni rossi*
1 onion	*una cipolla*
3 ripe tomatoes	*tre pomodori maturi*
olive oil	*olio d'oliva*
salt and pepper	*sale e pepe*

Hold the peppers over a naked flame or grill them briefly to peel. Cut each one in half, remove the seeds, rinse in cold water and dry carefully.

Fry the chopped onion in oil until it's transparent. Add the tomatoes, and after a minute or so put in the sliced peppers. Season, cover the pan and simmer, stirring occasionally, until the peppers are tender. *(Serves 4)*

CHAPTER NINE

CHILDREN AND BABIES

Most Italians love children. A family holiday in Italy can be a completely different experience to one in Britain: there's nothing more uplifting than finding that your children are universally accepted and admired wherever you go.

The concept of 'showing off' is meaningless in Italy and children are never accused of it. A baby in a pushchair will be greeted by all and sundry. You'll find that he or she gets into all sorts of conversations quite independently. Don't be alarmed if some grandmotherly figure finds herself unable to resist kissing your baby's bare feet – it's not unusual!

However, this friendly interest in your child can have another side to it. Italians believe in wrapping their babies up very warm. To us an Italian spring or autumn ranks as hot weather and we tend to allow the baby to go barefoot and lightly dressed. This will shock men and women alike in Italy and they won't be able to resist giving their opinion on the matter. The opening gambit is generally '*Oh, poverina!*' (poor little girl!), uttered in shocked tones. The whole thing can become a bit gruelling if your baby is at the age when he/she just can't resist taking off shoes and socks. Some people can be silenced by a quick riposte such as: *Non sente il freddo – è inglese* (he/she doesn't feel the cold, he/she's English), but with others you won't be so lucky!

A self-catering holiday can provide a perfect, sheltered introduction to foreign travel. If your children are too young to enjoy the 'total immersion' approach you'll be able to cook familiar food for them and stick, at least in part, to their usual routine. Older children can accumulate memories that they'll value for the rest of their lives.

Naturally, children accompany their parents to all the tourist attractions. However, if you go to a church, you should make sure they don't make too much noise – babies, as always, are the exception to the rule, as they are generally considered to be beyond reproach. Climbing on ruins at archeological sites should be vetoed.

CHILDREN'S FOOD

If your children are at the 'picky' stage, you'll be relieved to know that hamburgers and other international fast foods have invaded all the large Italian cities. Pizza, still considered a 'young food' outside Italy, is available in some form or other almost everywhere. You'll find fish fingers (*bastoncini di pesce*), hamburgers (*gli hamburger*) and pizzas made by Findus in the freezer cabinets of most supermarkets. Fresh sausages can be fried and eaten in the same way as our own.

EATING OUT

Your children will be welcomed in restaurants and *trattorie*. Don't worry about making a little bit more noise than everyone else – people really don't mind. The baby is quite likely to be whisked away for a game in the kitchen, allowing you to get on with your meal. It's the sort of thing that we never allow in this country, but in Italy it's the norm. Revel in it while you've got the chance and don't be unnecessarily protective. Ask whether they have a children's menu (*un menù per bambini*). Most restaurants are quite understanding about young children's food fads. If they only want pasta followed by pudding or fruit that's quite alright, there's no obligation to order a full meal. If you've got a baby the cook will probably be willing to make a *pastina*. This is usually very fine pasta cooked in broth and served with parmesan. If it worries you, make sure that the broth is fresh and not made with a stock cube: *E brodo buono, o è fatto col dado?*

You'll probably come home longing for the English equivalent to the Italian bar – another place where your children will be welcomed. Bars cater for all ages – you can order whisky and soda for yourselves and ice-cream for the children.

SHOPPING FOR BABIES

You will probably decide to take supplies of the milk that your baby is used to. However, most chemists stock a range of powdered milks. One of the most popular is Evlac made by Dieterba.

Baby foods can be bought from most chemists and supermarkets. Traditionally the Italian baby's first taste of real food is *brodo di verdure*. It's made by boiling up a carrot, a courgette and a potato and then mixing the water that they were boiled in with a little ground rice. A lot of people do use instant baby foods but their price suggests that they are still considered something of a luxury. For example, a box of Milupa baby rice will cost you the equivalent of about £3. Baby foods made in Italy (Milupa is Swiss) are slightly cheaper. Dieterba is one of the principal manufacturers. Their version of baby rice costs about £2.50. They make the usual range of creamed cereals and vegetables and most of them are gluten free. With a sprinkling of parmesan on top and perhaps a drop of olive oil for the older baby they are really quite palatable.

Plasmon is another major Italian baby food manufacturer. They make a range of homogenized meats that are suitable for older babies. Two little jars of about 80g (3oz) each cost the equivalent of £1.50. Dieterba do much the same thing at the same price, and they both produce jars of homogenized fruit similar to Heinz at home. These cost about £1.20 for three jars of 80g each.

La pastina is the traditional food for slightly older babies (see under EATING OUT above). Served with a sprinkling of parmesan and a drop of oil it's delicious. You can use any small pasta to make your own *pastina* but Dieterba, Milupa and Plasmon all produce special baby pastas with added minerals and vitamins. Baby juices can be bought from chemists or supermarkets. You may prefer them to ordinary fruit juices which nearly always have added sugar.

TOILETS AND NAPPIES *(gabinetti e pannolini)*

Toilets are very variable in cleanliness, etc., and some of them are the simple hole-in-the-ground variety with a foot-rest at each side. Motorway stops usually have good facilities, including mother-and-baby rooms.

There's no need to overload your car with disposable nappies and babyfood. These can both be bought anywhere in Italy and you can often find familiar brands. Disposable nappies can be bought from the chemist *(la farmacia)*, the supermarket *(il supermercato)*, and sometimes from the sort of shop that sells anything from lavatory paper to oven cleaner, known as a *mesticheria* in Tuscany, or *una drogheria*. You'll usually be able to find Pampers, although the Italian brands such as Fissan and Lines are more common. On the whole they cost much the same in Italy as they would in this country.

BEACHES *(spiagge)*

Italian families usually escape the heat by going to the sea or the mountains. If you do choose a seaside holiday try to find out something about the beaches before you decide where to go. Places that would be sheer heaven on your own can be hellish with children.

Find out what the beaches are like and how easy they are to get to. At the height of the season the roads around seaside resorts can be very full. There's nothing worse than sitting in traffic jams between the beach and your holiday house when you should be in the sea. Italy has no shortage of beautiful sandy beaches and safe, shallow seas. However, some areas – particularly the islands – tend to have a sheer, rocky coastline, where the quietest and most beautiful beaches can usually only be reached by following a long and treacherous path down the cliffs. With a baby or young children it can be almost impossible to get to sea level, let alone get home at the end of the day! In the South the rocks are often volcanic and tremendously sharp and rough. Children will be in danger of scraping their knees and hands and there will be nowhere flat enough for the baby to crawl.

MOSQUITOES *(zanzare)*

Mosquitoes seem to love the taste of babies. If you prefer not to smother the baby all over in mosquito repellent take a length of fine net curtain and drape it over the cot. If you're still using a pram or carry cot an ordinary cat net will do very well. Otherwise, there's an appliance you can buy from Boots that repels them.

BABYSITTERS *(babysitter)*

If you're going to a tourist resort-style apartment on the coast, check to see if babysitting is available. Even if it is, you may not find it suitable for your children, particularly if the babysitter doesn't speak English. Some self-catering companies organize beach activities for children for some part of the day.

CHAPTER TEN

PRACTICAL HOUSEKEEPING

This chapter is designed to help you with the kind of practical, domestic troubles that can sometimes ruin a self-catering holiday. If you know how to get the appropriate help a domestic crisis can turn into an adventure. You can learn a lot about real Italian life by mixing with plumbers or electricians!

If you've booked your holiday house through an agency there will probably be a caretaker on hand to help with practical problems (see Chapter 5, WELCOME TO ITALY). You may even find helpful dual-language notices pinned up around the house. This will give it an institutional look, but when the loo blocks or the hot water system packs up you'll be glad of them. It's always worth the agent's while to keep the customer satisfied and so you'll probably find that eveything is in fairly good working order.

Problems are more likely to arise in houses that have been rented privately. There may not be a caretaker on hand to help you out and there's no guarantee, for example, that the house will have been cleaned properly before you arrive.

RUBBISH (la spazzatura)

The rubbish should be put into one of the black plastic bags issued by the council. In cities this will be collected from the pavement outside your front door every morning. In rural areas the system varies. You may find a huge, communal dustbin to dump your bags in.

If you're not sure what to do, ask a neighbour what the system is: Where should I put the rubbish? *Dove devo mettere la spazzatura?* When is it collected? *Quando portano via la spazzatura?* If you are staying in a town you may find your new, council issue rubbish bags stuffed into the mail box. If not ask: Where are the rubbish bags? *Dove sono i sacchetti per la spazzatura?*

LAUNDRETTE *(la lavanderia)*

If you need to go to a laundrette while you're on holiday, note that, in Italy, they are often closed during August.

LAVATORY *(il gabinetto)*

If the lavatory causes problems you may need to call the plumber. Ask at the local bar for *un idraulico* or look one up in the yellow pages *(le pagine gialle)*. If you have to ring him up you may well find an answerphone on the other end of the line. Help! If your Italian isn't up to it, it might be as well at this point to bolt to the nearest tourist office, where they'll be able to help you.

Once you've got hold of a plumber, tell him that the lavatory is blocked/doesn't work/is leaking: *Il water è bloccato/non funziona/perde l'acqua.*

CENTRAL HEATING *(il riscaldamento)*

If the central heating breaks down, find a plumber (as described in LAVATORY above), and say: *Il riscaldamento è guasto*; or The hot water heater has gone out – *Lo scaldabagno è spento.*

ELECTRICITY *(elettricità)*

If the lights suddenly go out you may simply have fused them by overloading the system: The lights are fused: *E saltata la corrente*. This is much easier to do in Italy than in England, because the Italian system – as is the case in other continental countries – has a trip-switch. This tends to be hyper-sensitive, and it will trip if you so much as consider putting the washing machine and the iron on at the same moment. Try to find the fuse box before you fuse the lights!: Where is the fuse box? *Dov'è la scatola dei fusibili?* It may well be in a communal cellar, so keep a torch somewhere handy. Fuse boxes in communal areas are often locked: Where is the key to the fuse box? *Dov'è la chiave della scatola dei fusibili?* When you open the box you'll see a range of switches. The trip switch is usually either red or black. It will be switched in the opposite direction to everything else and will need switching back.

For problems with the electrics that you can't solve yourself, you'll need to find an electrician (*un elettricista*) in the same way as described above for finding a plumber (see LAVATORY above).

GAS *(gas)*

Gas cookers can either be connected to the mains supply, or run off a gas bottle (*bombola del gas*). If it's the latter, make sure you have a spare early on, otherwise it's bound to run out just as you're preparing the evening meal. It's usual to leave a full one for the next occupant, but this doesn't invariably happen! You'll have to pay a deposit (*deposito*) on the cylinder. If the house or apartment is connected to the mains, and you discover a gas leak, leave the windows open and call the plumber (see LAVATORY above). Tell him there's a leak: *C'è puzza di gas.* The gas meter is *il contatore del gas.* Gas cooker is *il fornello a gas.*

CHAPTER ELEVEN

WHILE YOU'RE IN ITALY

SURVIVAL SHOPPING

This A–Z section covers essential items that are sometimes difficult to find. Some of them can be bought from a large supermarket (*supermercato*), but if you don't have one near you, this list tells you where else you can find them.

A–Z

- antiseptic (*un antisettico*) For minor wounds and stings go to the chemist (*la farmacia* – see below under medicines)

- asprin (*aspirina*) From the chemist

- calpol (children's liquid paracetemol) From the chemist. The Italian version is called Tacciperina. It's the same as ours, only much sweeter

- can opener (*un apriscatole*) From the ironmonger (*negozio di ferramento*)

- cleaning materials (or household goods of any kind) can be bought from a shop called the *mesticheria*

- corkscrew (*un cavatappi*) From the ironmonger (*negozio di ferramento*)

- contact lens liquid (*la soluzione per le lenti a contatto*) is sold by the optician (*l'ottico*), although you may find that some large chemists stock it as well. You can usually buy familiar brands. Hard contact lenses are *le lenti a contatto rigidi*. Soft ones are *le lenti a contatto morbidi*

- contraceptives (*contraccettivi*) are sold by chemists. Some large supermarkets sell condoms (*preservativi*) as well, but they are twice the price in Italy that they are here

- dental repairs You'll have to go to the local dentist (*dentista*) – ask in the tourist information office where to find one. Take your E111 with you – it should entitle you to free treatment

- kitchen equipment The ironmonger (*negozio di ferramento*) not only sells kitchen equipment but also other tools

- medicines The chemist (*la farmacia*) is a hushed, important place with an air of the hospital about it. Apart from medicines, it sells first aid materials, baby food, toothpaste and foods for special diets. The pharmacist (*farmacista*) is trained to diagnose minor illnesses. If you can show him what's wrong, so much the better. He has the authority to sell a lot of medicines that we can only get on prescription in this country. Take an old box or bottle with you if you can, this will help him to give you what you need. He can even administer an injection if he sees fit. If the chemist can't treat you he'll give you the address of the nearest doctor on duty. The chemist has a large green or red cross outside. When it's closed the name and address of the duty chemist (*farmacia di guardia*) will be displayed on the door

- nappies, disposable (*pannolini*) can be bought from a chemist, or in some cases the *mesticheria*

- plasters (*cerotti*) from the chemist

- tampons (*i tamponi*) (often known by the trade name 'Tampax') are sold by the chemist

- underwear From the haberdasher's (*merceria*). You'll probably pay less at a department store or at the local market. Men's underpants are called *mutande*, knickers are *mutandine* and a bra is *un reggiseno*

- watch batteries (*una pila per l'orologio*) can be bought at a watchmaker's shop (*orologiaio*).

LOCAL SERVICES

BANK *(la banca)*

Banks are open for five hours each morning Monday to Friday. The exact times vary from bank to bank, but it's usually from one of the following: 8.15 to 1.15, 8.20 to 1.20 or 8.30 to 1.30. In the afternoons they are usually open until 3.30. On islands and in other remote areas the bank may only open for a few hours each week.

Allow yourself plenty of time when you need to go to the bank, since cashing a cheque takes a long time. You'll need a passport as identification for cashing a cheque, even if you're using Eurocheques with a cheque card. Make sure you join the queue for the *cambio* – if you wait in the wrong queue you can waste a lot of time. Sign the cheques in front of the clerk, then don't be dismayed if everything, including your passport, is bundled up and thrown into a tray to be taken somewhere else. At this point, you move on to the queue for the *cassa* (cashier's desk). Even if the rest of the office is open-plan, the cashier will probably be sitting behind a bullet-proof glass screen. This won't deter him from having long chats with his regular customers.

Despite the informal atmosphere – bank clerks are often quite informally dressed – security is high. You will probably have to come and go through a special glass booth fitted with electric doors. From the street it will probably be marked *entrata* and from inside the bank *uscita*. You need to press a button to get into the booth. You won't get out again unless you press the other button. Should they suspect your intentions, the bank clerks can keep you trapped in there like a bee in a bottle.

Larger cities usually have an exchange bureau (*cambio*), which is often at the railway station. You can change money and travellers cheques outside normal banking hours, and often until quite late at night. However, you'll have to pay a high commission. Hotels change money too, even for non-residents, but the rate of exchange is usually very poor.

TRANSPORT

If you are without a car, or want a change from driving, there are other ways of getting around, although none of them are fast. Public transport is heavily subsidized and is thus very cheap. In large cities you may enjoy yourself more if you abandon the car and take the bus. There's nothing worse than trying to find your way around the one way system with an inadequate tourist street map. Even if they are slow, local buses give you the chance to relax and take in your surroundings.

Public transport is usually half-price for children under fourteen, depending on the Azienda Municipale Trasporti, and babies ride free. There will be any number of baby addicts among the other passengers to help you pass the time.

BUS AND TRAM (*l'autobus e il tram*)

Buses are well used in Italy, and some cities have a tram system as well. Buy your tickets from the tobacconist (*tabaccaio*), newsagent (*giornalaio*) or bar before getting aboard. If you plan to use the bus frequently, it's worth buying a book of tickets. There's an automatic ticket punching machine at the back of the bus, which prints the date and time of your journey onto the ticket. Should an inspector get on, nothing but a stamped ticket will satisfy him. Travelling with an unstamped ticket amounts to fare evasion and results in a fine.

Get on at the back and off again either at the centre or the front of the bus. However, buses are often too crowded for this system to work. If you have trouble getting off shout: *Permesso!* ('mind your backs'). If the bus moves on shout even louder: *Devo scendere!* ('I've got to get off').

There will be some information about the bus service on the bus stop itself (*la fermata*), and the buses carry a list of the stops on their route. The bus station (*il capolinea*) will often have an information point. In the villages, the bus usually stops by the bar and the person in the bar acts as an informal source of information.

In large cities there are buses with a red, diagonal line through the number on the front. These take a different route to those with the same number but with no line through the number, so beware.

Useful phrases

How can I get to . . . ?	*Come posso arrivare a . . . ?*
What time does the bus leave?	*Quando parte l'autobus?*
How long does it take to get to . . .?	*Quanto ci vuole per arrivare a . . . ?*
What time does the return bus leave?	*A che ora partono gli autobus per tornare?*
Where is the bus stop?	*Dov'è la fermata dell'autobus?*
Where can I buy a bus ticket?	*Dove posso comprare un biglietto per l'autobus?*
Can I get off please?	*Posso scendere per favore?*

COACHES (*i pullman, le corriere*)

For journeys of moderate length coaches are often quicker and more reliable than trains. The tickets are cheap and the coaches are usually quite comfortable.

Make sure that you get on the right sort of coach, since there are several types that go to the same destination starting a more or less the same time. The *rapido* generally takes the fastest route and doesn't stop along the way. The *diretto* will divert to stop in the larger villages *en route*, while the *locale* stops far more frequently.

TRAIN *(il treno)*

Trains are very cheap, clean and comfortable, and the stations can be exciting places. As with the coach, make sure you get on the appropriate train: the *treno locale* stops everywhere; the *diretto* stops at all the main stations; the *espresso* is a long-distance train that stops at principal destinations only. The *rapido* is the equivalent of our Intercity, and you should book your seat in advance. You'll often find that all the seats are first class and you usually pay a supplement on the *rapido*. However, with the relatively low cost of the tickets, it's a small price to pay for a fast and comfortable journey. *Super rapido* trains (TEE – Trans Europe Express) run between the principal cities such as Rome and Venice, Milan and Bari, etc. Some of these trains have special names: the Milan–Rome is called L'Ambrosiana, and Milan–Bari is called L'Adriatico, for example.

Most of the international and long-distance trains have restaurant cars where you can order a meal in quite formal surroundings. On other trains a trolley usually comes round with drinks and snacks. At large stations you can buy a packed meal especially for the journey. This can be quite elaborate – a hot pasta dish, roast meat, fruit, and a quarter bottle of wine. When a long-distance train stops someone always materializes with a barrow of ice-cold drinks. He runs feverishly up and down the platform shouting and selling his wares to anyone who can manage to squeeze a hand out of the slit windows along the corridor.

Allow yourself plenty of time to buy a ticket, there's bound to be a long queue. The ticket system is complex and each transaction takes a long time. You can buy your ticket on the train, but there will be a considerable penalty to pay in addition to the price of the ticket. If you're buying a return ticket, be absolutely sure that it won't expire before you intend to come back. Tell the ticket clerk when you'll be returning: I want to come back today/tomorrow/in a week's time/in a month's time: *Voglio tornare oggi stesso/domani/fra una settimana/fra un mese.*

195

Useful phrases

How much would a ticket for . . . cost?	*Quanto costa un biglietto per . . . ?*
A single ticket to . . . please	*Un biglietto di sola andata per . . . per favore*
A return ticket to . . . please	*Un biglietto di andata e ritorno per . . . per favore*
Second class	*Seconda classe*
First class	*Prima classe*
Do I need to pay a supplement on this train?	*Devo pagare un supplemento per questo treno?*
What time will we arrive in . . . ?	*Quando arriviamo a . . . ?*
Have we still got a long way to go?	*Ci manca molto ancora?*
What is the next stop?	*Qual'è la prossima fermata?*

TAXI (*taxi*, pron. 'tassì')

These are generally cheaper than in Britain. In large cities there is usually a yellow metered cab service. Taxi ranks are marked with a 'T' and can usually be found outside bars and stations, and in the city centre. There is also a twenty-four hour radio cab service that you can ring. Look up the number in the yellow pages (*pagine gialle*). If you have to catch a train or plane in the small hours, book a cab the night before.

The driver will ring various supplements on to the meter, either at the beginning or end of a journey. These relate to the number of passengers and the amount of luggage. He should have an explanatory list of charges on board if you want to see it. Cabbies expect to be tipped – about 5% is appropriate. It's a good idea to memorize the cab number in case you leave anything inside.

Some journeys are charged at a standard rate. This is

usually true of the trip out to the airport. Ask how much it will cost before committing yourself.

Most cities have a host of un-metered mini-cabs – avoid these if possible. Be particularly wary of the drivers who hang around outside stations and airports. They aren't registered and can't use the official taxi rank. They are quite unscrupulous about over-charging. If you have to use a mini-cab, ask the driver how much it will cost before he starts slinging the luggage into the boot!

TELEPHONE *(il telefono)*

The SIP (central exchange) found in most large towns makes telephoning very easy. There's no need for small change. You don't even need to know the number or the code you want if you're making a national call – they keep all the directories and some foreign ones too. Present yourself at the desk and tell them where you wish to call. (This isn't important if you're making a call within Italy, but they need to know if you're ringing abroad.)

There may be a queue, but eventually you'll be allocated a numbered cabin. (N.B. the light won't come on until you go inside and shut the door.) Your call will be metered and the cost will register continuously on a digital screen above your head. When you finish the call, go back to the desk and they'll give you the bill.

Public call boxes are scarce, but you can always make calls from bars, restaurants, main railways stations, tourist offices and central post offices. Look for a telephone symbol on the wall outside. Beware of using hotel phones, they always charge a large commission.

You may need tokens *(gettoni)* – these often turn up in your change as they also serve as normal currency. The newer phones take ordinary 50 and 100 lira pieces. Put the money or tokens in before lifting the handset. Be prepared for a completely different set of tones: the ringing tone is only slightly longer than our 'engaged' signal, which is a frantic 'pip-pip-pip' in Italy. There are also phone cards *(carte telefoniche)* available from newsagents and petrol stations.

Telephones are organized under different towns, cities and villages. You'll need to know roughly where someone lives before you look up their number. The yellow pages *(pagine gialle)* are similar to our own and form part of the general directory.

See also CONTACT WITH HOME, later in this chapter.

NEWSPAPERS *(giornali)*

These are bought either from the newsagent *(giornalaio)* or street kiosk. The principal national newspapers are *La Repubblica* (published in Rome and with a left-wing stance), *Il Corriere della Sera* (published in Milan and is slightly right of centre), *Il Manifesto* (an independent communist paper), *Il Paese Sera* (published in Rome and slightly left of centre), *La Stampa* (socialist) and *L'Unità* (the official Communist Party daily). *Espresso* and *Panorama* are the main official news magazines with sections on politics, science, art and music.

TV AND RADIO *(la televisione e la radio)*

You are unlikely to find a television in your holiday home unless you do a house swap. Most bars have one, however, and it will be switched on for most of the day. If there's a football match on it will be surrounded by a cheering crowd.

There are innumerable independent channels – some are devoted to broadcasting American soap operas and films, others concentrate on game shows, some go in for soft porn and others for TV auctions. The equivalent of our BBC is called RAI. There are three main channels and each one is controlled by a different political party. RAI 1 is Christian Democrat and has mainly 'light entertainment', although the news at one o'clock probably has a larger audience than any other news programme. RAI 2 is socialist and RAI 3, which is devoted to documentary and political analysis, is broadly communist.

The situation is much the same on the radio. There are any number of local and independent stations. RAI has three channels: RAI 1 is roughly equivalent to our Radio 4, and RAI 3 corresponds approximately to our Radio 3.

You can catch up on world news in English by listening to the BBC World Service, in Italy you'll find it between 9MHz and 18MHz.

HEALTH

This section deals with the minor but aggravating things that can go wrong health-wise when you're abroad. For more serious matters, see LOCAL SERVICES earlier in this chapter, and EMERGENCIES (Chapter 12).

STOMACH UPSETS AND DIARRHOEA

Upset stomachs can be caused as much by too much sun, as by the food, although children tend to double their fruit intake – and adults their wine intake – abroad. A day indoors, largely asleep, often works wonders.

In the case of diarrhoea, it's important to drink plenty of fluid, as dehydration can set in very quickly in Italy's hot climate. This is especially important for small children, and if you have an electrolyte powder (such as Dioralyte) with you, make use of it. If a bout of diarrhoea lasts for more than 24 hours you should seek medical attention.

Kaolin tablets are an excellent corrective for diarrhoea caused by excess fruit and wine. As soon as the worst is past, make sure that you – or whoever is suffering from diarrhoea – eats some solid bready food. Lomotil (which you will have to bring with you, for it is on prescription) is the best medicine for stomach upsets caused by bugs in the water or bad hygiene.

If your stomach is sensitive, avoid anything with milk, cream, yoghurt or mayonnaise in it. A change of diet itself can cause problems. Don't buy meat that has been displayed in the sun or in fly-infested areas.

KEEPING COOL

The evaporation of sweat from the skin is the body's way of cooling down. Drink plenty of liquids (preferably water) to prevent dehydration. Children may protest that they're not thirsty, but ensure they drink at regular intervals. Take a *siesta* in the hottest part of the day. Wait until the late afternoon to sight-see or go to the beach.

SUN

Don't imagine that you can emulate that wonderful olive or mahogany tan that Italian people develop – unless your skin is fairly dark already. Being in the sun can make you feel wonderful, but over-doing it can cause permanent damage to your skin. Not only can you get nastily burned, but a link has now been established between sudden, intense exposure to sun and skin cancer. You're most at risk if you have fair or freckled skin which burns before it tans, or if you have fair hair or light-coloured eyes. Protect yourself by:

- choosing a sunscreen that protects against both UVA and UV
- reapplying sunscreen at regular intervals (water and sweat will wash it away)
- using sunscreen on cloudy days; the sun is just as harmful through cloud
- gradually building up the amount of time you spend in the sun; never stay in the sun until your skin goes red
- avoid sunbathing in the middle of the day when the sun is at its strongest
- covering up when you're walking round in the sun
- wearing a good pair of sunglasses to protect your eyes.

For bad burns – on adults or children – when the skin peels and the flesh turns scarlet – visit the pharmacy for advice. You may be recommended lanolin to smooth thickly on the affected area. Keep covered up and try to keep in the shade as well. Swim with a shirt on until the burns have healed completely.

SUNSTROKE

This makes the eyes look yellow, and is accompanied by headache and sickness. A day in bed in a darkened room, drinking juice usually cures it. Broken veins in the eyes are one temporary but unpleasant form. Polarized sunglasses help to prevent this.

SALMONELLA

Be careful – hot weather makes bacteria breed at a fearful rate. Raw poultry is the main cause. Putting them down on boards which are not then scrubbed before being used for something else, or using the same fork to poke or turn birds, and then to move other food. It is this sort of thing that transfers salmonella from raw poultry back to cooked poultry. If poultry is basted with marinade it must them be heated thoroughly again. Never serve poultry in the unwashed marinade bowl – although this seems natural when barbecuing in the garden.

STAYING SAFE

A few final tips to ensure that your holiday is happy and healthy.

- never let children in the water without at least one capable swimmer to keep an eye on them
- always check that the water is deep enough before diving
- stay away from animals that might bite or scratch – you risk catching rabies
- avoid riding motorbikes and bikes unless you have the right protective clothing
- make sure you know who to contact in an emergency (see EMERGENCIES, Chapter 12).

DRIVING

The Italians have a reputation for reckless driving. They certainly drive more noisily than we do – no inhibitions about using the horn – but their national accident record is probably much the same as our own. The important thing is to remain unflustered by sounding horns and wild gesticulations.

ROADS

Italy is a mountainous country, and its roads represent remarkable feats of engineering – you will often find yourself driving through tunnels or hugging the cliff face thousands of metres above the sea.

The motorway network is well developed – the road numbers are prefixed with 'A' (*autostrada*), and the signs leading to them are green. With the exception of a few sections that act as city ringroads, all motorways charge tolls (*pedaggio*). Milan–Rome, for example, costs about £20. Take a ticket from the machine when you go onto the motorway. When you come off you'll be charged according to the miles you've travelled and the size of your car. Most motorways have plenty of service stations where you can fill up with petrol, buy a meal and souvenirs. Many have picnic areas.

Main roads are prefixed with the letters 'SS' (*superstrada*).

In the country many of the back roads aren't surfaced, and this makes driving very bumpy and dusty at best, but with ice and snow they become really treacherous. At high altitudes, it is sometimes obligatory to use snow chains during the winter. Mountain passes often have to be shut, and there's usually a notice at the foot of the pass telling you this.

HIGHWAY CODE

This is not an exhaustive list of the rules of the road in Italy, for that you should get the appropriate pack from your motoring organization. What follows is an outline of some of the more immediate things you'll have to know when driving on Italian roads.

On a three-lane motorway you are expected to travel in the centre lane. The inside lane is for slow vehicles and the outside one for overtaking.

SPEED LIMITS

These vary on motorways. Assuming that your car engine is larger than 900cc, you can travel at 130km/h (80mph) at weekends. During the week, the limit is reduced to 110km/h (68mph). On other roads, the limit is 90km/h (56mph), and in towns it's 50km/h (31mph).

WHITE LINES

A solid white line is the equivalent of our double line. It means no overtaking.

GIVING WAY

Always give way to traffic coming from the right – this is particularly important at roundabouts. Trams always have priority.

TRAFFIC LIGHTS *(i semafori)*

Traffic lights pass straight from red to green – giving everyone the opportunity to hoot furiously if you happen to miss them. An amber light always passes to red, so slow down when you see it. Overhead lights can be difficult to see against the sun, but there's always an additional light low down on the pole – a help if you're at the front of the queue.

ROAD SIGNS

These are some of the more common ones:

rallentare	slow down
divieto di passaggio	no entry
tenere la destra	keep right
sosta autorizzata	parking
sosta vietata	no waiting

sottopassaggio	underpass
pedoni	pedestrians
parcheggio	car park
nebbia	fog
gelo	frost

DRIVING SAFELY

- Drinking and driving is illegal in Italy.
- Seat belts must be worn by the driver and the front seat passenger at all times.
- Your headlamps should be converted for driving abroad by using either headlamp converters or beam deflectors.

TRAFFIC POLICE *(vigili urbani, polizia stradale)*

The traffic police patrol in pairs on motorbikes. Don't expect to get away with anything because you're a foreigner, and make sure that you have your Green Card, registration papers and driving licence *(patente)* at all times.

PARKING *(parcheggiare)*

The Italians have a rather cavalier attitude to parking. They often draw up across the pavement at a rakeish angle, making life impossible for pedestrians. Illegally parked cars risk being towed away. If this happens to you, contact the police by dialling 116.

If you return to your car to find it blocked in by another vehicle, check that the keys aren't in the ignition. It's quite normal to leave the keys in or the handbrake off, so that your car can be shunted out of the way if necessary.

When you go to a car park, you'll often be expected to leave the keys with the attendant. He will park the car and move it around as necessary to make space for other vehicles. He'll expect a tip for his services, especially when he allows you to leave the car even though there is no official space for it.

In large cities there are usually teams of unofficial parking attendants who make an income by moving illegally parked cars around just ahead of the traffic wardens *(vigili urbani)*.

Probably not something to get involved in if you're not local!

In many cities there are 'blue zones', where parking is restricted between 9 a.m. and 2 p.m., and between 4 p.m. and 8 p.m. to cars displaying a disk. These can be bought at the local tourist office.

The Automobile Club d'Italia (ACI) has carparks in most large cities. They charge about 800 lira (about 40p) for the first hour, then more for subsequent hours.

PETROL *(benzina)*

Self-service garages are less common in Italy than they are in Britain. The pump attendant will often clean your windscreen as a matter of course, and will be happy to check the oil and tyres. There are some 24-hour garages and others that have 24-hour pumps but no attendant. These pumps take paper money, but not if the notes are too crumpled.

There are two grades of petrol: *super* and *normale*. Unleaded is *benzina senza piombo* and diesel is *gasolio*. You can either tell the attendant how much you want to spend, or the quantity you want to buy. A gallon is just under 5 litres.

Tourist coupons Tourists driving in Italy can buy booklets entitling them to reduced price petrol, reduced tolls and free breakdown service on major roads. The booklets are available to all foreign motorists, except those in hire cars, and can be bought from border posts, the Tourist Office, and motoring organizations.

There are four different booklets: *Italia* contains petrol coupons and toll vouchers which can be spent all over Italy; *Italia Centro* contains one petrol coupon redeemable in central and southern Italy, and petrol coupons and toll vouchers which can be spent throughout Italy. *Italia Sud* contains some petrol and toll vouchers which can only be redeemed in southern Italy, and others which can be used anywhere in Italy. *Italia Sud, Basilicata, Calabria, Sicilia e Sardegna* contains some petrol coupons and toll vouchers which can only be redeemed in the areas mentioned, and others which can be used anywhere in Italy. Unused petrol coupons can be reimbursed up to two years after issue.

USEFUL PHRASES

Could you check the oil/tyres/water for me please?	*Può controllare l'olio/le gomme/acqua, per favore?*
Could you clean the windscreen?	*Può pulire il tergicristallo?*
Put in 20 litres please	*Venti litri per piacere*
Fill the tank please	*Il pieno per favore*

BREAKDOWN AND REPAIRS

If you need assistance on the road, dial 116. On the *autostrada* you can use the SOS telephones on yellow poles. The button with the monkey wrench on it is for mechanical problems, and the red cross is for calling an ambulance.

If you can't get to a phone, you'll probably be found by the traffic police. Holders of tourist vouchers will be towed to the nearest Automobile Club garage free of charge.

Labour costs less in Italy, so a breakdown will be less expensive than you might think.

USEFUL PHRASES

I've broken down	*Ho la macchina guasta*
Is there a garage near here?	*C'è un garage qui vicino*
I've got a puncture	*Ho una gomma a terra*
Will it take long?	*Ci vuole molto per farlo*
Will it be expensive?	*Sarà molto costoso?*
accelerator	*l'acceleratore*
handbrake	*il freno a mano*

CONTACT WITH HOME

MAIL *(posta)*

Post offices have a round yellow sign outside with the letters 'PT' on it. If you don't manage to get to a post office (*l'ufficio postale*) within opening hours, you can also buy stamps (*francobolli*) from tobacconists. But try to post letters and cards at the post office rather than using the red boxes (*la cassetta delle lettere*) in the street as the Italian postal system can be rather erratic. Delivery can be slow, especially of postcards (*cartoline*); if it's important pay a little extra and send a letter by airmail (*via aerea*) outside the EC, or registered mail (*posta raccomandata*) or express delivery (*espresso*). You can also send telegrams (*un telegramma*).

If you are staying in an old apartment block (that is, not purpose-built), or one that you are hiring or borrowing from a private owner, post is usually delivered to a series of named boxes in the main hall. If you are expecting any letters, make sure that they are sent 'care of' the owners, because if it only has your name on it, the postman will be defeated and take it away again. Be sure that you get the post box key from the owners – there's nothing worse than knowing that your letter is there and not being able to get at it without sacrificing the damages deposit!

POSTE RESTANTE *(fermo posta)*

If you don't know the full address of where you are staying, you can have mail sent to you care of the local post office. Letters should be marked *ferma posta* followed by your name in capital letters, and then the full address of the post office. You'll need your passport to collect mail, and there may be a small service charge.

TELEPHONE

To phone the UK dial 00 followed by 44 (the UK code). You can make international calls from the *Posto Telefonico*

Publico (PTP) where you pay the clerk afterwards (see LOCAL SERVICES earlier in this chapter for more details.)

To find a pay telephone in Italy, simply look for the yellow disc with the outline of a receiver or telephone in black. Most cafés and restaurants display them.

There are also international telephones in larger post offices. (See also LOCAL SERVICES earlier in this chapter for more details about the telephone system.)

If the phone isn't a pay phone, and you want to make more than one call, you may have to tell the owner, since the line will usually cut out after you put the receiver down. He or she will reconnect the line for each new call you make.

CHAPTER TWELVE

EMERGENCIES

EMERGENCY TELEPHONE

Dial 113 in an emergency and ask for *un'ambulanza* (ambulance), *polizia* (police) or *pompieri* (fire engine).

USEFUL PHRASES

Is there a telephone nearby?	*C'è un telefono qui vicino?*
There's been an accident	*C'è stato un incidente*
Call a doctor!	*Chiamate un medico!*
Dial 113	*Chiamate il centrotredici*

HOSPITAL, DOCTOR AND DENTIST

It's very important to take your E111 with you to Italy. This will entitle you to free national health service treatment under EC regulations. Without it you'll find yourself paying an exorbitant amount, particularly if you have the misfortune to need a dentist. (See Chapter 4, GETTING READY.)

The local chemist will be able to tell you where to find a doctor or chemist. If there isn't a chemist, ask in the shop or bar: Please could you tell me where I can find a doctor/dentist? *Mi può dire dove posso trovare un medico/un dentista per favore?*

POLICE

There are several types of police in Italy, each with its own distinctive uniform. The *carabinieri* are the military police, who deal with public order. They also keep an eye on traffic, and can be seen patrolling the motorways on powerful motorbikes. They wear long black leather boots and black breeches, and they carry guns. The *polizia* are a detective force, although they also operate speed traps on major roads. The *finanza* is the 'financial' police force, concerned with tax evasion, fraud, and customs and excise. They also stop cars to check their tax discs. They wear grey uniforms with yellow flames on the epaulettes.

LOST PROPERTY AND THEFT

Bag snatchers and pickpockets make a healthy income out of unwary tourists. Look out for boys on mopeds – they'll often snatch the bag off your shoulder as they pass. Gipsy children are the most common pickpockets. They work as a team, crowding round you and distracting your attention while they clean out your pockets. You'll often seen people walking around with a car radio in one hand. Italian cars all have removable radios – the result of too many smashed windows and too much theft. Try to conceal your radio in some way if you have to leave it in the car.

If you are robbed, go to the *questura* (police station). Take your passport with you – if it hasn't been stolen. There will be a long wait and a good many forms to fill in, but you may get some of your possessions back, even if you lose the money. If you've lost your passport, go to the nearest British consul (see below).

LOST TRAVELLERS CHEQUES

When you get travellers cheques you get a record sheet and instructions about what to do in case of loss or theft – it really is wise to hang on to these and keep them safe. You must keep a record of the cheque numbers, and of ones that are used so that you know exactly which ones are lost. If not, a lost cheque is like a lost banknote – gone, irreplaceable.

You will have been given a form with instructions about what to do in case of loss. For American Express, contact the nearest office, and the cheques will be replaced after much form-filling. If your travellers cheques are from a bank or building society and you don't have the instructions about what to do, go to an Italian bank, or a branch of any UK bank and they may be able to put you on the right track. The tourist office in a large centre may also have some useful addresses. You can also use the international directory enquiries to find out the number of your bank at home and phone direct.

LOST CREDIT CARDS

The minute you discover your credit card is missing, phone the 24-hour 'Lost and stolen' number. Report it at home, not in Italy (apart from American Express, see below).

The 'Lost and stolen' numbers for the UK are:

- VISA   00 (wait for high tone) 44 604 230230
- ACCESS   00 (wait for high tone) 44 702 362988
- AMERICAN   00 (wait for high tone) 44 273 696933
  EXPRESS   (or contact any local American Express office)

If you have no cash dial the operator and ask for a reverse charge call (*una chiamata a carico del destinatario*). The credit card company will accept the call.

CONSULAR SERVICES

Don't approach the local British consul for services that would be provided by the police or local hospital at home. It's not their job – nor have they power – to skip over local regulations and get you a special service. But they can advise on transfer of funds, provide lists of local doctors, lawyers and interpreters, give advice and contact relatives in the event of the death of one of your party, and give advice if you are arrested while in Italy. They can issue emergency passports – needed in Italy to change money – and in particular to get back into Britain without passing through a detention centre; they can also help if you are destitute – no money, cards, contacts or prospects; no means of getting home – particularly for the under 16s; and general catastrophe. But they cannot help with the mishaps of the holiday that turns out to be a nightmare, simply because of a score of small things that just go wrong.

INSURANCE

As a general rule, make sure you take your insurance policy with you and any emergency telephone numbers they supply you with. If you are going to make any sort of claim, keep all receipts, etc., carefully, and (in the case of theft or loss) make sure that you have made a report to the police or your claim may be void.

CHAPTER THIRTEEN

BUYING THINGS TO TAKE HOME

What you choose to take home with you will depend on whether you're flying back, driving or going by train – how much extra weight you can take, or are prepared to take. There are plenty of traditional things to take back.

CERAMICS

Decorative china bowls and jugs (*ciotola/scodella, brocca*) can be carried home safely in the back of a car. Look out for majolica (*maiolica*), a traditional and particularly pleasing pattern.

CHILDREN'S CLOTHES

If you have any spare cash you'll probably be tempted by Italian children's clothes. They cost more than ours, but they're very beautiful. It's not unusual to see an Italian toddler wearing a coat that you wouldn't mind having yourself!

FOOD AND DRINK

Everyday Italian things that you can take by train or air will turn into luxuries the moment you get home. Buy a good lump of parmesan, olives, capers and a string of dried chilli peppers or garlic (*parmigiano, olive, capperi, peperoncini, aglio*). Get some macaroons (*amaretti*) or some dried truffles (*tartufi*).

You could stow away a few litres of good olive oil (*olio d'oliva*) in the back of the car. Sometimes you can buy a demi-john of it directly from the farm – make sure that the top is secure before you leave. You'd never be able to find such good quality oil at the same price in England.

It's well worth taking wine (*vino*) home, even if you have to pay duty on it. You won't necessarily save a great deal of money, but you'll be able to take something back that you'd never find at your local off licence. Before you decide on a wine make sure that it will stand the long journey: *Questo vino si sciuperà in viaggio?*

You may have developed a taste for the local liqueur. You're unlikely to be able to buy it in England, so take a bottle back with you. (However, it's sometimes the case that a drink that tastes delectable on holiday loses its magic when you try it again at home.)

UK CUSTOMS ALLOWANCE

ALLOWANCES FROM DUTY-FREE SHOPS
- 1 litre spirits, liqueurs etc over 22%
  or
- 2 litres not over 22% (sherry, sparkling wine)
  plus
  2 litres still wine
  OR
- 4 litres of wine only

ALLOWANCES FROM ITALIAN SHOPS
- 1.5 litres spirits, liqueurs etc. over 22%
  or
- 3 litres not over 22%
  plus
  5 litres still wine
  OR
- 8 litres of wine only

GLASS

If you are staying in Venice you can buy traditional Venetian glass (*vetro*) that has been blown in the traditional way. You can see this being done if you visit the island of Murano, where the craftsmen create a world of decorative glass.

HANDICRAFTS

Wickerwork in particular is made on Sardinia.

JEWELLERY

Visit the Ponte Vecchio in Florence, where you'll find a mixture of modern and antique wares to choose from. If it's coral (*corallo*) that you're after Naples is the place. There are several large workshops to the north of the city where you can see the raw coral being transformed into necklaces, cameos and bracelets.

KITCHEN EQUIPMENT

There's plenty of useful kitchen equipment that can be difficult or more expensive to buy in England. If you've got used to using a tall, Italian pasta pan (*la pentola per pasta, il pentolone*), you may want to bring one back with you. The cheapest ones are coated in brightly coloured enamel – you can often buy them at markets. The huge colanders (*lo scolapasta, il colapasta*) especially designed for draining pasta are useful as well. You can also buy *espresso* machines (*la macchinetta espresso*).

LACE

The lace (*pizzo*) made on the island of Burano in the Venetian lagoon is famous.

LEATHERWORK

Florence is famous for its leatherwork (*pelle*). You can visit the leather warehouses and find soft leather bags, wallets, belts, a pair of shoes or leather boxes. None of these things will be cheap, but they will cost less than they would in this country, and they'll be beautifully made.

POTTERY

If you've got the car you'll probably be tempted by the magnificent terracotta pots (*vasi di terracotta*) and urns (*urne*) that are sold all over Italy – they cost about half as much as their English equivalents. Statues (*statues*) and wall plaques (*placche*) are usually on sale at the same places.

WOODWORK

Fine marquetry furniture and boxes are made in the South.

Index